A Hellish Place of Angels

A Hellish Place of Angels

Con Thien:
One Man's Journey

Daryl J. Eigen

iUniverse, Inc.
Bloomington

A Hellish Place of Angels
Con Thien: One Man's Journey

Copyright © 2012 by Daryl J. Eigen

All rights reserved. No part of this book may be used or reproduced by any means, graphic, electronic, or mechanical, including photocopying, recording, taping or by any information storage retrieval system without the written permission of the publisher except in the case of brief quotations embodied in critical articles and reviews.

iUniverse books may be ordered through booksellers or by contacting:

iUniverse
1663 Liberty Drive
Bloomington, IN 47403
www.iuniverse.com
1-800-Authors (1-800-288-4677)

Because of the dynamic nature of the Internet, any web addresses or links contained in this book may have changed since publication and may no longer be valid. The views expressed in this work are solely those of the author and do not necessarily reflect the views of the publisher, and the publisher hereby disclaims any responsibility for them.

The cover photo © by David Douglas Duncan as well as his other photos © used herein were taken in September- October 1967 at Con Thien, Vietnam. Harry Ransom Center (HRC) The University of Texas at Austin.

ISBN: 978-1-4759-3212-6 (sc)
ISBN: 978-1-4759-3213-3 (e)

Printed in the United States of America

iUniverse rev. date: 06/26/2012

To my mother,
Pearl Rice Eigen

From this day to the ending of the world,
But we in it shall be remembered—
We few, we happy few, we band of brothers;
For he today that sheds his blood with me
Shall be my brother.

—William Shakespeare
St. Crispin's Day speech in *Henry V*

Contents

Preface ix

Acknowledgments xv

Introduction xvii

Prologue xxi

Part I   Boot Camp 1

Part II   Journey to the 'Nam 23

Part III   The 'Nam 41

Part IV   Into the Zone 103

Part V   Con Thien: "The Meat Grinder" 147

Epilogue 171

About the Author 175

Appendix I   Operations 179

Appendix II   Awards and Decorations 183

Appendix III   Chronology of My Tour 187

Bibliography 193

Preface

The Brown Case

In the summer of 1998 I flew from my home in the San Francisco Bay Area to my hometown of Milwaukee to help my brothers and sisters move my eighty-nine-year-old mother from her house to a more manageable condominium. I didn't know that this was the beginning of a long journey of rediscovery. My mother, Pearl, had lived in her house for more than twenty years. The house was in a nice neighborhood on the east side of Milwaukee. It was not too far from Lake Michigan and was within easy walking distance of the University of Wisconsin–Milwaukee, where all of her kids at one time or another had been students. It was the house my father had died in after being married to my mother for more than half a century.

The house was a white Milwaukee bungalow, an odd and modest home that originated and proliferated in Milwaukee after World War II. The Milwaukee bungalow was a small home that had the attic lifted to allow a new family consisting of a war veteran, a war bride, and a baby or two to live in the upstairs of a parents' home. Cute dormers brightened the love nest. My mother had lived in the house alone for ten years since my father died and rarely went upstairs after having both her hips replaced. Mom loved gardening. The house and yard, mostly the yard, had won the Mayor's Award one year for being one of the most beautiful in Milwaukee. She was very proud of this distinction.

We all showed up at the house at various times that Friday in early June, including Donna, my twin sister; Barry and Beverly, the older set of twins; and Charles, my younger brother. Everyone except me lived in Milwaukee or its environs and in the months before the move had been working diligently to help Mom get things ready. Throughout her life our mother had saved everything, so there was plenty to sort through, throw out, and give away. The things Mom cherished had more emotional value than any worldly worth. I had already made it clear I wanted nothing, for a number of reasons, not the least of which was I did not want to have more to carry.

That afternoon, when most of us were present, Mother came out of the bedroom and into the dining room, which was cluttered with boxes and artifacts of a lifetime. Her silvery white hair framed her face. The light from the kitchen gave it shiny highlights. She was now only four feet eleven inches—shrunken with age. She had a sad smile on her lined face, and her large bright brown eyes were teary.

She said, "I have something for you." Since she didn't say, "Don't tell anyone," I wondered what it was. She always tried to give me things secretly, saying, "Here, take this, don't tell anyone." I most often refused, since I am not particularly a collector.

I assumed she treated all the kids the same way, although I never checked. Conspiracy was one path to intimacy in our large family. I always felt special, even though there were five of us kids.

She went into the bedroom again and brought out one of my father's sales cases. It was a dusty and heavy brown, wide block of leather. I opened it by springing the brass-colored clasps. Inside was a collection of items from the time I was in the Marine Corps and Vietnam, including all the letters I had written home during my tour of duty. I had forgotten about them. There was also my boot camp graduation album, a large rolled picture of the battalion I went to Vietnam with, and a Marine Corps manual.

I checked the case further but couldn't find the medals and ribbons I had been awarded. Shortly after my return from duty in 1969, I had ceremoniously burned all of my uniforms and had proudly presented the medals and ribbons to my mother. I had thus divested myself of all tokens, symbols, and memorabilia of that period of my life.

I asked Mom where the medals and ribbons were. She said she didn't know. She was upset by this discussion and then said Barry had them. I was not ready to pursue this any further—or remember—and quickly snapped the case closed and carried it to my car.

Later that afternoon we walked my mother to her new apartment, and she said, "My life would have been perfect if only you had not gone to Vietnam." I looked at her sadly, and she added, "Well, of course you have more than made up for it." Her memories as a mother reading these letters may have been worse than mine having had the real experience.

After doing as much as I could, I left for San Francisco. As I carried the case full of letters, I felt as if I were carrying the remains of a young man, my former self, who had died in Vietnam. It overwhelmingly felt like my duty to honor that lost boy in some way. That boy was more the father of who I am today than was my real father. I had tried to suppress, ignore, deny, and blot him out for thirty years. Now it was time to face the horror and pain. The time was right to remember and to heal.

When I got home I placed the case in a prominent place so I would be reminded to deal with the letters. One day while looking at the case I called my brother Barry and asked him about my medals and ribbons. I felt my family had not honored my deeds, deeds that for some twisted reason I felt I had done on their behalf.

Barry eventually found the awards and decorations. He sent them to me via special delivery. They were jumbled and dusty, and some were missing. At first I thought this was disrespectful, but then I had an insight that the medals and ribbons represented so much pain that the family could not bear to care for them. They held the pain I could not feel.

Slowly, day by day, I confronted the letters. To help my recollections and to try and understand what my family had gone through, I researched my war experience in the library microfiche and archive files of magazines and newspapers of the time. In the rarely visited periodical section of the library, I found several references that pertained specifically to my unit and my experience. Some of the letters even referred to newspaper articles or had been sent with clippings enclosed. Later I researched the Internet for more material.

Doing historical research really helped put my experience into context. When I was in Vietnam I was just a boy on the ground, a "grunt." I was sent here and there without any explanation. I just went. I did not know why or even where "there" was. I was not aware of the importance of the battles I was in or some of the things that were said about them. After checking some history books, I found that I had been in several battles of note: the early battles of Khe Sanh (the hill fights), 2/9's armored thrust into the demilitarized zone (DMZ), and the siege of Con Thien, which marked the beginning of the TET offensive. Oddly enough, reading about the military history, strategy, and tactics was comforting and helped me make some sense out of what had happened. Overall, the journals and references provided a bigger picture and some proof of shared experience of the grotesque images and feelings I recalled.

I once saw a sweatshirt that said, "My life is a true story." That epithet seems somehow appropriate for this book. I am not sure what the truth is anymore. My memories have become clearer, but sometimes they change the more I think about them. In certain details the articles, my letters, the history books, and my memories do not agree. What is the truth? Memory is a strange thing. The past does not exist as I imagine it. The past is not stored in my memory like a résumé, and the linear flow I experience from moment to moment in the present is also absent. In my mind the past is a stew of images, feelings, sounds, and smells that come into my consciousness, sometimes at will and sometimes against my will. I have worked hard but not always successfully to leave the past behind.

No matter—the letters started to bring the memories back. Now that I have read and reread the letters, I have the sense there is something unreal about them. Some I do not remember at all, and some seem like they were written by another person, a stranger. On the other hand, I can always recollect some events with digital, crystal vividness.

A few of my memories have been told as stories. Some have been greeted with skepticism and disbelief, as war stories so often are. People believe a story well told conforms to the truth but is not bound by it. But mostly I did not talk about the war. For decades just the spoken word "Vietnam" would be such a conversation stopper that no one would dare mention it.

The letters are not the whole truth. As horrible as some of them are, they were bravely sanitized by a boy so his family would worry less. The articles from the *Sea Tiger* and the *Pacific Stars and Stripes* were clearly whitewashed to keep the morale high. We all know about the "truth" reported in newspapers and magazines.

I wonder about some of the facts reported in the letters, like the confirmed kill counts. I don't remember how they came about. We now know there was a tendency to exaggerate these numbers by the high command. Was I infected with this tendency? An article in the *New York Times* said 1.5 million North Vietnamese and Viet

Cong died in the war, compared with 185,000 South Vietnamese soldiers and 58,000 Americans (Mydans, 1999). Maybe the body counts were not exaggerated. In some sense it doesn't matter exactly how many people I killed. The unavoidable, unfortunate fact is that I killed many. For this I am filled with deep, profound regret.

Beneath this regret there was a fog that covered the horror. Beneath that fog was a sea of tears that I began to access as I got into the letters. Beyond the deep sadness, I started to realize I had locked away some of the most powerful experiences and lessons of my life and had failed to integrate them. A successful life and career were testimony to my having seemingly recovered from the war, but I had done so at the expense of a very important part of myself. Now I see that I was deeply damaged by the war, and my haunting dreams ruled the day and the night. Except for my children and wife Lucy, my postwar life now seems of minor significance when compared with what I found out about myself, life, and God in the war. Apparently I was not ready to understand what I'd learned until now.

With war and violence still a very prominent feature in everyday events, I decided to make the integration of my war experience part of my spiritual quest. With this intention I faced my feelings and memories to wring out the truth—not the social, political, or historical truth but the inner truth. In many ways Vietnam is the perfect war for this endeavor, precisely because it was the wrong war for the wrong reasons, at least for our side, or at least for me. The dark, bleeding suffering of Vietnam provides the essence of what war is precisely because it is not hidden by a noble cause, not shrouded by righteousness, and not cleansed by victory. By exposing my experience in Vietnam to the light of awareness, I hope to help further heal myself and possibly others from the affliction of violent struggle.

The truth is, this book is white gauze wrapped around a still messy and bloody wound.

Acknowledgments

I would like to thank the following people for their help and support: Suzanne for typing the letters and Jo Muilenberg for her editing skills. Molly, my daughter, gets the most kudos for reading a very early draft and giving me encouragement and some great input, which I followed. Tony and Lori, my son and daughter in-law, believed in me and put up with all my nonsense. Stephanie Eigen, the wife of my nephew, Sam, who is mentioned in my letters, gets my gratitude for enthusiastically reading all I gave her and still asking for more. To my brothers, Chuck and Barry; my sisters, Beverly and Donna; and my mother and father I give my deepest prayers and thanks for keeping the faith while I was in Vietnam and welcoming me home from that dark journey. Donna deserves all the credit for editing this text through her tears and giving me loads of encouragement. Thanks again to Chuck for reading it and for his heartfelt words. I also want to remember Mike Belfer, then husband of Beverly, who welcomed me home at the hospital with a brotherly hug. Sadly, he is now deceased. Bev was instrumental in driving me to publish the book so it could be read. Special thanks go to Ashlee Whitehead, my VA PTSD therapist, for supporting and encouraging me through this endeavor. I am grateful for Jim Coan's (former

Captain of the USMC and Con Thien Vietnam veteran) invaluable help. The world famous photographer David Douglas Duncan was kind enough to let me use some of the photos he took while at Con Thien in September and October of 1967 including the one used for the cover. Thanks to Linda Brisco Myers at the Harry Ransom Center for facilitating Mr. Duncan's permission. Finally, I want to thank Lucy Burwell Eigen for her love, so freely given, that made me want to finish this book and continue the process of healing.

Introduction

The Beginning of Violence

My family was extremely nonviolent. The first exposure I had to real guns was with my friend; let's call him Joe. We occasionally went hunting for birds. I remember killing my first bird, which was also my last. I saw the blue feathers explode with the shot. The blue jay was slaughtered. I felt awful. I had always identified with the blue jay because Jay was my middle name. I had killed one for no good reason other than sport. I never hunted again.

Joe and his older brother had a twisted sense of humor. One day I showed up at Joe's house. His brother, who was a precocious nineteen-year-old, was sitting on a chair holding a shotgun. I was seventeen. He started right in by asking where his hat was. I said, "I don't know and don't have it." His fury escalated quickly, but there was a funny grin behind his mask of anger. I didn't know what to think. He yelled, "Where is my hat?" and pointed the shotgun at me. I stood my ground. I was sure he would not shoot. He laughed. In slow motion I saw the gun go off, and something hit me hard in the belly. It hurt. I felt my stomach, and there was no blood. I pulled up my shirt, and there was a big red spot that was quickly turning into a bruise. At first I was confused, but then it became clear as he rolled on the floor laughing. He had shot me with a blank wad. Blank or not, it was the first time I had been shot. He could not stop laughing. I felt betrayed. I also felt rage. I wished he would die. In about six months, that wish came true. He was killed in a tragic head-on crash in Louisiana. He was the passenger, and he sailed through the windshield over a bridge railing and into a dry riverbed.

My father was a peaceful man and never served in the armed forces. He had a critical job deferment during WW II. Uncle Art, my mother's brother, was in the Bataan Death March. My Uncle Max, my father's brother, also served during WWII, but he would never talk about it. None were in the Marines. There were no family expectations that I enlist—quite the opposite. They were shocked and forlorn when I did.

I joined the Marine Corps at eighteen to "become a man." It was that simple and that complex. Before joining, I had a lot of fear. I was afraid to fight or get into any challenging situation. To cover this fear, I was angry and rebellious. It was also my chance to get back at my parents at the same time for all of the imagined abuses I had endured as an adolescent. My enlisting had little to do with patriotism and more to do with joining the adventure. My father had always said I was too smart for my own good. I certainly fulfilled that expectation. I had little to no comprehension of what I was getting into. My father also said about my rebelliousness, "Daryl, you are fighting with yourself." These words were more profound than I or my father realized.

Along with fighting myself, I ended up fighting different elements of the Vietnamese Communists. My experience in the Marine Corps and especially Vietnam was a little like boiling a live frog one degree at a time. Any faster and the frog would leap out. Each day it seemed I received the most I could handle, and each day it seemed it was more than the day before. I began fighting the dedicated but somewhat ragtag Viet Cong at the beginning of my tour in Vietnam in 1966, but by the end of my tour in 1967 the fighting had escalated into heavy conventional combat against divisions of well-trained and well-equipped North Vietnamese army regulars. Needless to say, my survival was in doubt at every turn.

Prologue

Exposure Therapy

We walked in a spread-out column with flanking elements. We walked using extra care and concern as if every one of us was on point. We walked as if it was our last moment on Earth. The air was laden with fear and expectation. It just felt wrong. I heard the crunch of the gravel road under my boot. I tried to hold down the nauseating and persistent idea of what a wrong move it all was.

Before getting very far, there was a large explosion at the front of the column. And so it began.

I listened for any foreign sounds, such as the rattle of an enemy canteen. The first mortar shells loudly started to walk down the road bank. One round landed between the Marine walking the flank and me on the road. In slow motion I was blown backward onto the road. Time slowed, and there was silence. I could not hear for a few seconds. I checked myself over and seemingly was okay. The Marine on the left bank screamed, "I'm hit!" I rushed to his side, yelling "corpsman" to no avail. He said, "Check my balls, check my balls." I took my K-bar and cut his pants. I saw a deep laceration and told him his jewels were fine. I put a battle dressing on his wound.

The air was filled with yells, screams, and whistles. Pandemonium broke out as the little brown-clad men pierced our column in many places. I saw a stream of NVA—North Vietnamese army—back up the road overrun a portion of the column. One Marine was firing his rifle but was not pointing it. He was just shooting into the ground. I yelled at him to shoot. He went down instead. A Marine ran by me with his hand held high, screaming, "My hand, my hand!" I stopped him and looked through his hand and saw the battlefield through the hole. I told him he would live and wrapped his hand in my last battle dressing.

I heard shouts from some Marines on the right flank when facing south. "Get him, shoot him!" An NVA soldier had broken through the underbrush. I raised my pistol and shot in an automatic, trained gesture. My Marine cohorts shouted, "You got him!" I walked over to see, and a black shroud protected my mind from the carnage of his face. A fellow Marine said, "He had an *ax* and you blew his face off." I was breathing very hard and shaking.

The therapist asked me to come back to the here and now.

We had marched to the Ben Hai River on a small dirt-and-gravel road with an armor-reinforced battalion (Second Battalion, Ninth Marine Regiment), looking to engage some elements of the multiple North Vietnam army divisions that were occupying the DMZ. The Ben Hai River runs east to west, from the South China Sea to the western hills and mountains and Laos. The river provided the northern boundary of South Vietnam and the southern boundary of North Vietnam. It was a river of mystical foreboding promising death and bad karma for lifetimes to come.

We had walked on the road on our terms on July 28, 1967, and spent the night near the river. The next morning we found ourselves returning on the enemy's terms. The armored vehicles had to stay on the road, as it was impossible for them to navigate the thick vegetation on either side of the road or in any reasonable vicinity. We, the infantry, had to provide a thinly veiled cordon of protection. Thus we were returning on the same road we had walked in on. Every Marine knew this was a bad idea. We were all mad and sick about what we knew was inevitable. It was July 29, 1967—my twentieth birthday.

More than forty years later, on a cool day in the fall of 2009, I was sitting with my Veterans Administration post-traumatic stress disorder (VA PTSD) therapist in her office at the VA hospital and clinic. She said, "You can relax now; take some deep breaths, and slowly open your eyes. We will do more next time."

There was a lot more to do. I had experienced some of the worst Vietnam had to offer, and much is recounted here in an effort to rid myself of my demons.

I had begun this journey more than ten years ago to reclaim my past but had not sufficiently addressed my PTSD. Continued exposure to the traumatic events is supposed to help.

I trust that one day it will.

Part I

Boot Camp

Yellow Footprints

I took a plane ride to San Diego and got on a Marine Corps bus to the Marine Corps Recruiting Depot (MCRD). It was early afternoon, January 27, 1966. It was hot compared to Milwaukee's frigid winters. When we got to MCRD a drill instructor (DI) got on the bus and started to yell at us. I thought it was funny. It seemed too put on to be real.

He had us get off the bus and line up on some yellow footprints. Somehow those yellow footprints brought the reality of the moment crashing down on me. The DI was not kidding. Someone had taken the time to actually paint yellow footprints for everyone who was on the bus. I realized that what I had done by enlisting was irrevocable. I had a deep insight in that instant that the only person I was hurting was myself. I also started to have an inkling that I was not as clever as I had thought. I grew up in that moment, and I thought I did not need anything else from the Marine Corps. But all of these thoughts did not matter. That was the horror of it. I was there—period. I had many more lessons to learn. The whole experience before me was beyond my imagination, as active as it was.

We marched—or, more accurately, were herded—from the assembly point to the reception barracks. The DIs quickly organized us to get our heads shaved and then to collect our government-issued clothing. They didn't pay a lot of attention to the clothing sizes on this first issue, so some of us were dressed in clothes way too big. It was all part of the program. We were rushed through the issue lines and marched to our huts while the DIs screamed at us the whole time. Every recruit was assigned to a bunk bed, top or bottom, and told to fall out. We lined up on the narrow street outside of our hut and started to hear what the Marine Corps thought of us "scumbag civilian maggots"—or just "maggots" for short. That night you could hear some boys sobbing in their beds.

See You in a Couple of Years
San Diego, California

Mom, Dad, brothers & sisters,
    Having a wonderful time. We eat well and live right. I am sure that I will be a good Marine, eventually. Surprisingly, I can say that my status here is excellent. However, the "esprit de corps" and "one for all" are not quite indented in my memory patterns. It seems to me like a college field course in group psychology, considering that we have to walk, talk, eat, sleep, and breathe together. See you in a couple of years.
    Love, Daryl

PS Mail would be appreciated.

Head House Mouse
Dear siblings,
    How is everything back north? The weather here is calm and blue. Mexico is only eighty miles south. I wish I could see the ocean, but I know it is there because occasionally when the sea is up, the salt smells faintly in the air. I dislike being regimented and losing my individuality, but by the use of my mental powers I was able to secure the job of "head mouse." That is to say I am boss of the two little mice who clean up the drill instructor's cabin. This might seem like a lowly job, but the "mice" are the ones who get promoted and possibly sent on to Stanford College to become an officer. See you. Write.
    DJE

PS Please tell Mom and Dad *not to send* cookies or candy. If you do, send in very small quantities, 1/8 pound or less. *None would be best.* Otherwise the drill instructors yell at you.

Fitting In
POSTCARD
2-5-66

Dear Mom & Dad,
    I am fitting in very nicely. I feel healthy and well. They, without too much trouble, have stopped all my bad habits, including drinking and smoking. Please write!!
    Love, Daryl

The Only Jew
2-6-66

After getting regimented toward the military program (have been here eight days), things are becoming easier and the days shorter. It is surprising how fast the time goes. I have made eighty-six new friends (my whole platoon) and we are oriented toward fast meals; early to bed, early to rise; and hard work. A week ago I couldn't imagine the work I do now. I am sure that in another week it will be even easier. They serve tremendous chow.

    Most of the time, I am too tired to even care. But I look past the sweat into the perfectly blue sky and let Mother Nature ease my woes. If only I could run in the green, fresh grass and have a glass of beer!

    Tomorrow is Sunday and I go to temple. Everyone goes to some kind of service on Sunday, even though one's holy day may be on Saturday. I am the only Jew in my platoon.

    I am sure that in at least eight months I will be hiking in the jungles hunting for VC with a loaded rifle. For now, we use an empty one. We are to learn every piece and every part. It is quite interesting, along with the lessons. For the most part we drill and exercise. You should see the obstacle course. Wow! I did a battery of placement tests and scored high. Got to leave.

Love, Daryl

The Vacation Is Over
2-9-66

The vacation is over; we have now started to work. And I mean work. Marching, running, and being bitched out all day are awfully depressing to some privates. As for me, I can take it ...
    Now that I am established in the program, things are getting easier. First thing this morning we ran a one-mile obstacle course with twenty obstacles. They consisted of twenty to forty foot ropes, ladders, and jumps with water. Also, a few eight-to-ten-foot walls with a three-foot-deep top making it difficult to scale. After each obstacle you have to do five pushups screaming your platoon number and then double-time to the next. When I finished I could not use my arms, but then we were ordered to run another quarter mile at full pace. I made it, feeling strong when I ended. Two weeks ago this would have literally killed me.
    By the way, Bev, I really am cut off from the outside world. I sat through five mail calls, and out of eighty-six privates in my platoon I am the only one who hasn't received a letter. Please write.
    Daryl

My Rifle Is My Friend
2-14-66

Dear Mom & Donna,
    Thanks for the two letters you both sent respectively. They really cheered me up. Things are going better than I expected, but still I work and work and work. By the way, I am writing this to you by penlight under the covers. I have really grown to like my rifle. It is

my best friend. This is what we were taught and, surprisingly enough, believe thoroughly. Also, we go to classes like history and interior guard. Chuck, you may be interested in hand-to-hand combat and bayonet classes where we scream, "Kill, kill."

Mom, it isn't really that bad. In one week from now we go to live at the rifle range for three weeks to learn to shoot. Also, our platoon won the physical training ribbon and will probably go on to win the drill, academic inspection, and honor ribbons, because it is a great platoon, gung ho!!!

Love Daryl

No Candy, Please
2-20-66

A lot has happened. Our platoon won the drill ribbon and the physical fitness ribbon. I personally came up with the highest preliminary knowledge test score in my platoon. Also, I am eligible for officers' candidate school.

The meals are great. For example, for breakfast we eat eggs, bacon, two pieces of toast, butter, jam, three milks, oatmeal, potatoes, and fruit, all at once, and the next day a different breakfast. For supper we have turkey or steak, fruit, milk, mashed potatoes, dressing, Jell-O, cranberries, salad, four different kinds of dressings, olives, celery, bread and butter, cake, pudding, peas, corn, all at once, and lunch is equally as big.

Also, we got our first paycheck (every two weeks). It was twenty dollars. My income tax return was fifty-five dollars, plus five dollars that I already had, which leaves me with plenty of money and no place to spend it. By the way, we have no leave, no TV, and "no" free time. Any spare time we do have I use to clean my rifle.

Don't send any candy, please. They make you eat it all at once.

Daryl

A Hellish Place of Angels

Hand-to-Hand Combat

Our platoon is using reconditioned Quonset huts, which have not been used since the Korean War. They are made of corrugated steel shaped into a half cylinder. Also, they are putting up hundreds of tents, holding thirty beds each. It looks like the war is really being stepped up.

Today in our hand-to-hand combat class we had practical demonstrations. I, unfortunately, broke one of my competitors' wrists, and the second one got his ear torn. Except for a sore jaw given to me by a six-foot-three, two-hundred-fifty-pound man (no bull), I came out all right.

We also went over a fifty-foot ladder. On the top rung, standing in the middle forty feet up, you have to jump for this two-by-four straight above you, roll over the top, and come down. Oooh! It's hard! We are going to the rifle range this Saturday for three weeks. One of those weeks will be maintenance. After that, only two more weeks and that's it for boot camp.

Daryl

Too Smart for My Own Good

Boot camp was thirteen weeks long. Shortly after I started, the Marine Corps introduced a nine-week version of boot camp for the next batch of new recruits to push more troops through. Already I was in the "old" corps. Being chosen as the head house mouse was a matter of selection by elimination. On the first day we stood in formation outside of our huts on the company street. The DI asked who knew Einstein's theory. I eagerly raised my hand, thereby making another grievous error; the first one was my being there. There were four of us out of the entire platoon who gave the correct answer. The DI then asked the killer question: Who was Keats? The DI walked slowly up to me, smiled a wry smile, tilted his head, stuck out his lower jaw, and said, "Softly whisper the answer in my ear, dear, so no one else can hear." I victoriously whispered my answer into the DI's ear: "He was a Romantic poet." I was so proud of how smart I was. I was the only one who knew or at least admitted he knew. I wanted to be recognized, and indeed I was. He angrily snapped his head around and screamed in my face, "What? You slimy faggot, you want to be romantic?" I was then given the job of the DI's head slave, called the head house mouse. The lesson: blend in, don't be different, and don't think. Oh yes, and never volunteer. It was already too late for me.

The only respite was temple. The Marine Corps took four things seriously: the Marine Corps, the country, Mom, and God. Temple was not a service but just a meeting held on Sunday where four or five of us from all of the training platoons were supervised by a navy chaplain, who was obviously not Jewish. We ate cookies and milk sent from a local chapter of some Jewish organization. My DI suspected this and confronted me one day, screaming at me that I only went for the wine. I stood at attention and just said, "Yes, sir!" as loud as I could. He was amused.

When my dog tags were issued they said my religion was "Jewage." I thought this was an ironic cross between Jewish and sewage. I never knew whether it was because the administrative Marines who made up the dog tags were deliberately prejudiced or just illiterate. I was not sure which was worse.

I was given special treatment. I had unfortunately distinguished myself enough to be made head house mouse. They knew I had some smarts so I had to help a few of the less able and two who could not read or write, during the knowledge tests. I worked out a scheme with my fingers for multiple choice. I would show a number of fingers for the right multiple choice answer. Three fingers would equal C, for example. Rather than silently copy the answer when I held up three fingers, they would loudly whisper, "Was that C?" Or they would lose their place and would loudly ask the question,

A Hellish Place of Angels

"What is the answer for 26?" If I silently answered that question, I would have confused the rest. It was all I could do to not laugh out loud. I was appreciated by the platoon.

Then the DIs found out from my application that I had been in a marching band in high school, playing the clarinet. I knew how to march. So they made me the official platoon whipping boy to add to my honors. They made me build a mound of sand. I had to run to the sand pile some distance away and run back with buckets of sand extended at arm's length.

After the mound was built I decorated it with white stones. One of the DIs made me name it Hebe's Hill. Nobody envied me. As the platoon drilled and practiced marching on the asphalt-covered parade grounds, I would stand at attention on my mound until the platoon made an error, which was quite often. I was then ordered to do twenty-five, fifty, or one hundred or more squat thrusts, with or without pushups, depending upon how egregious the error. It was the military version of yoga sun salutations. My hands would create two deep indentations in the dirt, sometimes halfway up my arms. In some sick way I actually enjoyed this exercise, and I earned the respect of the platoon.

The obstacle course was actually called the "confidence course." This was not a euphemism. Before boot camp I was not a fighter. As tough as I thought I was, I had a lot of fear of fighting. The obstacle course did boost my view of my abilities, but what motivated me more was my greater fear of the DIs. I was very surprised at how fast my body stepped up to the challenges and how well I did in hand-to-hand combat.

Marine Corps boot camp was, for me, very effective. It put me into my body and pulverized my civilian ego. I was becoming a Marine and turning into a warrior. By not being in my head, I was able to conquer my fear. By getting out of my own way, I was able to let the intelligence of the body protect itself in hand-to-hand combat.

Bigger and Stronger
2-23-66

Dear Donna,

    Hi. You'll never recognize me when I get home. I feel a thousand times bigger, stronger, and healthier. We live in a hut with twenty-eight men, and four left us today, two to prison and two to sick bay. Glad you're still at home.

    Daryl

PS Please send me some info on Vietnam, considering I'll be there in three months. However, I'll be home before then.

Pep Talk
2-23-66

Chuck,

    I hear you haven't been getting out of bed. You mean you're that gutless that you can[1]t even move one foot out of bed? Just try running three miles in the morning and another in the afternoon with twenty pounds on your back. It's hard but you do it.

    We started out with eighty-six original privates in our platoon. We now have seventy of those originals. Some are in jail; the others are in fat man's farm (a special program for those out of shape) or sick bay. Today we lost four more.

    It would help to get a high school education because the dumb ones even in the Marine Corps are fairly well educated. I am not trying to give you a pep talk, unless you are thinking about enlisting when you are older. Marine boot camp is hard—very, very hard. The food is good and the air is clean, but, man, it's work. Getting up at 4:30 a.m., exercising, eating, obstacle course, classes, marching, eating, running, marching classes, eating, rifle cleaning, snapping in, showers, classes at huts, and then the rack (bed) at 8:30 p.m. Quite a day and no time for horseplay.

    Daryl

Pep Talk Report
2-28-66

Dear Dad,

    I wrote to Chuck before I got your letter on the very same problem you discussed. Also, please do not use postcards if you do write. The DIs read them. Today I found out that I probably will get a month's training at ITR (infantry training) and four to six months in Okinawa, which is a jumping off place for Vietnam. In another week we go to the rifle range. See you maybe in another three months.
    Daryl J.

Helping the Other Half
3-20-66

I just got back from two weeks at the rifle range and I qualified. This gives me a medal. Also, yesterday was the hardest day we had. We ran a slow jog nonstop five miles uphill, and then we took our canteens full of cool water and dumped them out without a drink. Then we came to MCRD by bus, got off, moved into tents, ate lunch, and then went rope climbing and crawling on our bellies in full gear for an hour and a half. We then assembled and ran three miles in twenty-plus minutes, in step, full gear, repeating very loudly the calls of the drill instructors. At the end or near the end, half the platoon was helping the other half. But our platoon made it 100 percent. We then went to supper, showers, and hit the racks. Today, Sunday, was one of the easiest.

    By the way, I graduate in ten days, if I pass the few tests, physical and mental, coming up. No problem—the time here went incredibly fast. In fact, it seems like only yesterday that I left Milwaukee. I will be home in four to six weeks from now. Before that, I, as a Jew, on April 4, get leave for the night to go to a community center for Passover. Also, while at infantry training I will get a weekend pass that I will spend in LA.

DJE

Marksman the Hard Way

At the rifle range I had trouble qualifying. This was a huge problem. Every Marine's main job is to carry a rifle. Every Marine is a marksman. To provide extra motivation the DI made me collect rifles with my arms in front of me. People just kept stacking them up on my outstretched arms, one on top of another in a precarious heap. They asked me how much an M14 rifle weighed. I shouted, "Nine point one pounds, sir, without sling, magazine, and ammo, sir!" I was counting. I did not think I could hold more than ten rifles. I kept walking and each Marine laid his rifle on the stack. It was a game to see who would drop a rifle first. The person putting the rifle on top, or me, dropping the whole load. It was a sin to drop a rifle. It was impossible for me to win. I just tried to make a good showing. The stack was fourteen rifles high before I collapsed. That night I cleaned a lot of rifles.

While this increased my motivation, it did not improve my aim. The DIs started a ritual with me to teach me windage and elevation, two concepts important to hitting the target. Windage corrected the sight from left to right to compensate for wind. Elevation corrected up and down. The idea was to shoot in a tight cluster, and then you could adjust the cluster to the bull's-eye by so many clicks of windage and elevation. In a way it was like tuning an instrument.

The windage and elevation ritual would begin with me standing at attention. All of the DIs at one time or another would then punch me in the stomach and I would have to correct their aim to target

A Hellish Place of Angels

my solar plexus. They would admonish me not to fake it. They could tell and it would be much worse if I lied. "Two clicks up and one click left, sir," I would yell to correct their aim. By now my stomach was rock hard, but I was very good at helping them target my weak point. They would stop when I was doubled over.

On qualifying day I was still having trouble. It was hot and I was nervous. I was not doing very well. At five hundred feet I could barely see the target. Sweat was rolling into my eyes. The primary DI came over. He looked pissed. He had two bottom front teeth missing. He said he had had them pulled to hold his cigar better. He said nothing but took my hand into his mouth and bit my trigger finger like it was the end of a cigar he was going to bite off. He cracked the nail and drew blood. I was sure he had broken the finger. He said calmly through his cigar, "Now try and squeeze the fucking trigger." It hurt so much it was impossible to jerk the trigger. I qualified.

Toward the end of boot camp, I was confronted by this DI and one other. They showed me a bag of candy from somewhere and asked if it was mine. I yelled, "No, sir!" He screamed, "Are you a faggot?" I yelled, "No, sir!" The tall, younger DI struck me in the throat with a karate chop. It bent me over and scared me. He said I was lying. I wasn't, but I could tell this was not about the candy or about being gay, which I wasn't. It was either about my being Jewish or because they had finally realized I was a smart ass. In any case, they did not want me in their Corps. I had no options. If I fought them and by some chance won, I would be sent to jail. If I fought them and did not win, I would be hurt and sent to jail. If I cried and begged for mercy I would have washed out or have been beaten and washed out. I decided, for whatever reason, to just stand at attention and take it. They beat me for a while. Each time they knocked me down I would pick myself up without a whimper and stand at attention. They eventually stopped.

I forgot any notion of being an officer as I now knew this was about my survival and nothing else. And yet paradoxically I passed on a chance to sidestep the war: the next day I was asked if I wanted to go try out for the Marine Corps Band as they knew I played the clarinet. I stupidly thought I would miss all the action if I did. And I would be playing without any medals on my chest if I did. So I didn't. I wanted to become a warrior—in other words a "man"—even at the potential cost of my life. I was still deeply self-destructive. In any case it was a young man's folly.

Once a Marine, Always a Marine
4-6-66
Camp Pendleton, California

Well, I am finally a Marine and the improved conditions are amazing. I am at Camp Pendleton for basic infantry training for only fifteen days. Then I am pretty sure I get a thirty-day leave. Today is Sunday. We get to lie around, and next weekend we pull liberty. Now, instead of a twenty-four-hour day we have an eight-hour workday. We still live in those huts, but we have fewer people per hut and have wall lockers.

I imagine you have heard that I will be going overseas in July as operations and communications on-the-job training connected with the FMF (Fleet Marine Force) Ground Forces.

    DJE

Roll on Your Back and Wiggle
4-15-66

As you were, people, on that last letter. My info on being home in "fifteen days" was bum scoop because I found out I will be going to basic specialists training (communications operations) from two to eight weeks.

A Hellish Place of Angels

From there I can take leave for thirty days and then report to ship overseas, but I will tell you more about that when I get home. The training I am getting now is not discipline but rather infantry tactics and techniques. For example, yesterday we crawled on our bellies and elbows for four and one-half hours. I have bruises all over. While crawling, we came across barbed wire that was one to two inches off the ground. We then had to roll on our backs and wiggle under ten inches of it on our shoulder blades and buttocks using our rifles to let the barbed wire slide down our bodies. I suffered ripped pants, lost buttons, and a torn shoe. We also eat at least one meal a day in the fields (C rations out of cans), walking or running at least twenty miles a day. However, this weekend we will probably have shore liberty and I will probably go to Los Angeles for my first fling.

See you soon.

DJE

A Jew in the Gas Chamber
San Diego, California

To Charles & Donna,

What's new? Sorry haven't been able to write. Today I went through the gas chamber. They used tear gas in great quantities. For example, when we got in and were told to take off our masks and sing the Marine Corps hymn, big Marines were crying, choking, trying to get out, quivering on the floor in spasms trying to breathe. Some even knocked their heads against the wall and stomped their feet, drooling on the floor. If anyone put their mask on early, the instructor tore the mask off and either broke it or threw it out. When we were told we could leave, people ran, pushed, and shoved. All this commotion, but with scuba diving lessons under my belt I was able to calmly observe and only cough a little. When it came time to leave, I let everyone run out ahead of me and then quietly strolled out. After all, a Jew in a gas chamber has to keep his cool!

Tomorrow we go on bivouac! We have been eating C rations for more than two weeks. Boy, are they getting bad! At first they were a novelty. Last week we gave a demonstration to some brass in night tactics, including firing illumination mortar rounds and semiautomatic fire at tanks. It looked sharp. Also, we have fired the BAR (Browning Automatic Rifle) and will throw grenades and fire the 3.5 rocket launcher.

Yesterday and the day before we were on shore liberty. Boy, did I get plastered. I rented a motel room next to Disneyland with two heated swimming pools, television, stove, and air-conditioning. I am enclosing some pictures taken one week apart. The two with the cigar in my mouth (I was drunk) were taken yesterday, grrrr!

I outpost from infantry training this Friday and start my specialist training next week. No more physical. Now to the mental.

Bomping, stomping, death, and destruction. USMC.
Daryl J.
Gung Ho!

PS Bullshit.

Being a Marine

We were playing at war. It was necessary and it was fun. A group of us went to Disneyland. I felt torn between being a kid and thinking I was an adult. It was a strange brew of feelings. Being a Marine does not automatically make you a man. I was still a boy despite the warrior garb.

Pogey Bait
5-3-66
Camp Pendleton, California

B & B Eigen,

Living conditions are a lot better. I am not a boot or even a trainee but I am now really a Marine. I am stationed in Schools Battalion, Camp Delmar, Area 16. This weekend on base liberty I went swimming in a fabulous Olympic-sized diving pool. We were allowed shore liberty, but I was too tired to go. Also I took up eighteen holes of golf on the officers' golf course. Needless to say it took some doing considering we also got in for free. Three of us walked down there and a fourth man who could and did play made our foursome. He was dressed in civvies and we did not know he was an officer. However, without any intention on his part to let us know, we hit upon this fact on the seventeenth hole. It was embarrassing for us because we did not give him the respect his rank deserves and we were off limits. We just treated him like a friend. He was a good head.

Tonight I saw a flick. I will have the opportunity to go every night. We work from 8:30 a.m. to 4:30 p.m., and from 4:30 p.m. to 12:00 midnight is base liberty, plus shore liberty every weekend. How about that? Also, I am now living in barracks where we can smoke and eat pogey bait (candy). There are Coke machines all over, wall lockers and footlockers, things we were never allowed to use before.

I am in casual now, an institution developed since the draft was started. It has been impossible to keep up with the overload of men. Casual might last up to two months but I doubt it and from here I go to four weeks of specialist training in operational communications. The physical training still exists because this is still the Marine Corps. However, "they" know it takes aptitude to be chosen for this school and we are delayed from boot leave, so they treat us like permanent personnel. After my leave I will be going to West Pacific duty as my permanent duty station.

Gedunk

Pogey bait is candy you could get at the "gedunk"—a navy term for the ship's store. I was told a pogey was a derisive name for a young sailor that older sailors would find attractive on long voyages. According to the Internet it is a Chinese word Marines used for prostitutes when in China. Thus, pogey bait was used to snag prostitutes or whatever. The implications of the language we all used so unconsciously were mind blowing.

Combat Swim

7-11-66
Camp Pendleton, California

I arrived safely at Staging in preparation for Vietnam. I reported into training on the Fourth of July, and I am now in my fourth day of training. So far we have had the combat swim test (swimming with full gear on and diving off a tower). I passed, but many did not. Also, yesterday I received three shots in my arm (two with guns and one with the needle) before I was aware of what was occurring. The training is much like ITR (infantry) where we all run and are issued rifles and gear. Sergeants, corporals, and lance corporals are all going through the same training and sleep in the same billets. If they can do it, it must be easy. At the moment we are in the field phase of our training out here in huts in the middle of hills and mountains thirty-five miles from nowhere, and that nowhere happens to be Camp Pendleton. I'll be going over on the first of August and reporting to Okinawa. I then report to Da Nang, Phu Bai, Chu Lai, and I will be assigned to the Third Marine Division, Ground Forces, Fleet Marine Force.

    DJE

A Hellish Place of Angels

Western Union Telegram
Ten dollars from David F. Eigen in Milwaukee, Wisconsin, to PFC Daryl J. Eigen at Camp Pendleton, California

The Old Corps
7-28-66
Camp Pendleton, California

And here I thought infantry training was the hardest physical training I had yet to endure. How wrong I was, for now we do what we did in infantry training only with a radio and body armor. However, I am pretty much in shape now and presumably I need not sweat what there is to come. I am now up for lance corporal, but it seems I do not have enough time as a PFC. In two months I will have the required time, however; I might get it sooner, considering the job I am doing now requires a corporal or sergeant.

In the "old corps" one could not make sergeant in less than five years. I have a chance of making it in less than three years. Absolutely unheard of before 1964. However, rank is immaterial to me because here I get rank as it comes, and this is the best place in the Marine Corps to make it. Since I've been here, I have been through some very ingenious training, like the VC village. Also, in the past month because of administrative mistakes I have been forced to take all my shots twice over, amounting to many sore arms. Since I have been in the corps I don't know how many times I have been inoculated against cholera.

Love, Daryl

Victor Charley (VC) or Vietcong Future Flash
The VC village was a flash into the future. Huts with grass thatched roofs and dirt or bamboo floors provided the dreamscape of what was to come. We pulled maneuvers around and through the village

with "VCs" popping out of holes and snipers firing blanks. Because the village belonged to the Marine Corps we didn't get to blow it up or burn it down. But soon we would get our chance.

The Marine Corps is special and in my way I was proud to be part of it.

Harvey Keitel, the famous actor and former Marine who went to boot camp at Parris Island rather than San Diego as I did, summed up in 1998 the values of the Marine Corps on the *Charlie Rose* show on the 223rd anniversary of the Marine Corps. The essence of what he said is paraphrased in the paragraph below.

We were challenged physically, mentally, spiritually, and above all challenged to endure. We learned to work as a team and to respect the Marine Corps tradition. We learned through these challenges that we could overcome any obstacle and accomplish any goal. The Marine Corps develops a spirit and an esprit-de-corps in us young men that enables us to prevail in any circumstance and on any field of battle.

"… the tradition and history of the Marine Corps proves it."

Later in combat we learned from experience that we were not fighting for glory, we were not fighting for our individual survival, we were not fighting for abstract concepts like freedom, or capitalism, we were not fighting because of anger or revenge, and we were not fighting because we were ordered to. We were fighting with and for our brothers in blood, we were fighting to rejoin our families and to provide an opportunity for our mothers to see us again, and we were fighting for the right to be proud of being a Marine. We were not fighting for God, but we all prayed for his intervention on our side and on our behalf. Our fidelity to our country was a given but it was still hard to comprehend how fighting in a distant land was protecting our country. Most of us never gave these issues a second thought.

Maybe that is part of the reason I didn't care very much about what people thought about Vietnam when I returned home.

A Hellish Place of Angels

Being in the Marine Corps is a life-changing experience and it is true what they say: once a Marine, always a Marine. It is a little like being Jewish. In either case, you are born to suffer, endure, and intimately know war.

With this background, I prepared to go to war. Going to war, especially Vietnam, did not only alter one's life, it altered one's reality. War is in a different dimension. If one survives war and returns to the normal space-time dimensions of mortal beings, one is forever partly outside the flow of events, as is an actor on a stage.

Part II

Journey to the 'Nam

Daryl J. Eigen

3rd Battalion 26th Marines Patch

Alone and Scared

I finished radio school, took my thirty days' leave at home, and reported back to duty at Camp Pendleton, where I was put into staging in preparation for going to Vietnam as a replacement. After completing staging I was sent instead to a Special Battalion Landing Team (SBLT) that trained as a unit to go to Vietnam. With this battalion I experienced a sense of togetherness and purpose that was new to me. This feeling, as with all my feelings, was soon to be shattered.

The SBLT was Battalion 3/26. A Marine Corps battalion is composed of four line, or infantry, companies and a headquarters and service (H&S) company. All totaled, an infantry battalion consists of about one thousand men. A line company is divided into platoons, which are divided into squads, and then into fire teams. A line company conducts combat operations in the field, while the headquarters company supports the Marine companies. The Third

A Hellish Place of Angels

Battalion line companies took their letters from the alphabet and were known as I, K, L, and M companies, or India, Kilo, Lima, and Mike, using the radio-operator designations for the letters.

I was a radio operator in 81mm mortars (81 millimeters is the bore size of the mortar launcher, a relatively mobile, high projectile weapon). "Eighty-ones," as we were affectionately called, are always part of the H&S (headquarters and service) company. However, as a radio operator I was part of a forward observer team attached to line company Kilo. There were two of us—the forward observer, and me, the radio operator. We reported to the company commander and went everywhere the company did and sometimes a little further.

The original Third Battalion, Twenty-Sixth Marine Regiment (3/26) was part of the Fifth Marine Division that fought during WWII. The 3/26 colors were folded and the battalion was disbanded from the roles of the active Marine Corps on March 5, 1946. However, in response to increased United States involvement in the Republic of Vietnam (RVN), 3/26 was once again activated at Camp Pendleton, California, on June 1, 1966.

During the predeployment training the official designation of our unit was changed to Battalion Landing Team (BLT) 3/26. Various supporting elements were added, such as artillery, amphibious vehicles, engineers, corpsmen, and motor transport, increasing the size of our battalion with more Marine and navy personnel. On September 4, 1966, the BLT combat unit boarded ship and sailed for the Western Pacific (WesPAC) to become part of Special Landing Force.

When we left port there was a throng of parents and sweethearts saying good-bye. I had neither and felt very alone and scared. My bravado disappeared with the prospect of what was ahead.

We steamed to Hawaii, on to Okinawa, and then to the Philippines, where we received jungle training. The waters of Vietnam beckoned us with an inevitability that created a thick tension of impending doom.

Loose Lips Sink Ships
9-4-66
Oceanside, California

Today is Saturday. All of BLT 3/26 (Battalion Landing Team, Third Battalion, Twenty-Sixth Marine Regiment) is leaving except headquarters & service company, and that is the company I am in. We leave Tuesday the sixth of September 1966. I am sorry but I can't say the ship or our ultimate destination, but our first stop could possibly be Hawaii. Our platoon has trained hard together and we are tight. The day before yesterday we had a beer bust in the field where everyone got inebriated. They said there was an ulterior motive to see how the troops would act under the influence—we all passed the test, but just barely. My ankle is better now. However, it did not keep me from any of the training, which, indeed, was difficult and more arduous than any other training I was forced to go through. However, it was well worth it. I have pulled some fabulous liberty in the past weeks and spent a lot of money. I have probably done everything there is to do.

We are going aboard a small aircraft carrier where there is more room than an ordinary transport.

Tell Chuck that I saw his friend at the enlisted man's club (that used to be twenty-one to drink but now is old enough if you can look over the bar). The club is sponsoring live bands and pretty [women] so we showed the club how Milwaukee drinks and dances.

I am enclosing my new address. Although it is shorter, it is complete and I will be going a lot farther west than California.

    PFC DARYL J EIGEN
    3rd Bn 26th Marines
    H & S CO. FPO
    SAN FRANCISCO, CA 96602

Tell everybody I think of them. Please write. My letters will be painfully slow due to inability to get letters off of ship until we reach a port.

Love, Daryl

Paradise
Postcard
USS Arizona Memorial
Pearl Harbor, Hawaii
9-15-66
USS Valley Forge

Barry & Barb Eigen,
Paradise—I am only sorry I can't stay longer. I'll send souvenirs to everyone when I get to Okinawa.

Love, DJE

Heaven
Postcard
Waikiki Sunset
9-15-66
USS Valley Forge

Mom & Dad, Bev & Mike,
This is a place from heaven. The water blue—warm—crystal clear.
Love, Daryl J.

Beer Bust
10-4-66

I received your letter, Mom, but I must say things seem to be the same at home. I find it hard to imagine because every day is filled from 5:00 a.m. to 2:00 a.m. I rarely get more than three to four hours sleep a night, but surprisingly enough I am used to it and now have the ability to catch up at any time, any place. I see so many new things, places, and people every day that what I write in my letters is not even an outline.

For example, the other day as part of our training we had a beer bust for H & S Co. down by the beach. We had beer galore with barbecued steaks by the ten pounds with potato chips and salad. Everybody got roaring drunk and stuffed, including the officers. I rented a boat with another buddy and we went water skiing on the ocean outside of Okinawa. It was great jumping those huge waves and then coming back and having more beer and rubbing elbows with the brass. The party ended with throwing all officers, staff NCOs (Noncommissioned Officers), and NCOs in the water, an old USMC tradition.

Love, Daryl

The Meaning of Firmament
At this time I was happy in the Marine Corps. I was about to embark on an incredible adventure and had the feeling I was at the beginning of an odyssey.

I will never forget the stars over the Pacific Ocean. The night was so dark with the white glowing wake of the ship (the *Valley Forge*) in those vast waters. With no moon, the heavens were shining bright enough to make clear the meaning of firmament.

Echoes of WWII
10-4-66

Family and adjacent relations,
Right now I am sitting outside the island complex called Okinawa. We are about a mile out because there is no port and the waters are too shallow to accommodate a ship this big. Every picture of islands and

A Hellish Place of Angels

the ocean is not accurate. It is a thousand times more beautiful. Let me try to describe Okinawa. It has rolling green hills with sandy blond beaches and white crested green waters licking her shores. A few junks are floating in the bay and two cargo ships are anchored a little way off shore. The sky is dusted with white clouds and is an impeccable blue.

We have been sailing for two-and-one-half weeks now after stopping in Hawaii for liberty and seeing Wake Island and Iwo Jima. Wake and Iwo were terribly depressing. After days of "water, water everywhere and not a drop to drink," we were coming close to Wake. In anticipation, I awaited the miracle on a catwalk near the bow. On the loudspeaker the captain announced that we were passing the historic Wake Island, not more than ten miles starboard. I was looking in that exact direction. Ten miles at sea is nothing.

Well, I looked again and I saw it. It was a green shaded wafer floating on a cup of tea and if you should add lemon, it would sink. The highest point on the island is two feet. After this disappointment, I waited a week later for Iwo Jima, the place where the Twenty-Sixth Marines (my outfit) placed the flag on top of Mt. Serabachi at the cost of thousands of Marines. Again I waited and again I was completely shaken. You can see around Iwo Jima five times; it is about four square city blocks big (or rather small), and Mt. Serabachi is a mere hill. This incongruous piece of land sticking out is a monument to man's meager methods.

But Okinawa is beautiful and Hawaii was paradise. We will be off-loading here for a couple of weeks and then will proceed to the task at hand. My long tedious days on ship were spent doing physical exercise (by order), reading, and playing cards and dice. I was quite lucky on the whole trip and remained far ahead of my needs.

I am glad to hear everyone is okay, including the dog, but I am a little disappointed in Donna not going full-time to college. If there is any need of money, I think I can swing fifty dollars a month.

Love, Daryl

Rank
10-4-66

Today has been something else. It was a very memorable day. October 3, 1966, started very bad. I was late for formation and I missed chow, but as I was standing in company formation I heard my name called out. Someone pushed me forward and all of a sudden I was marching facing the captain. He handed me a piece of paper and congratulated me. I made lance corporal.

Thus promoted, I found out that I had the absolute minimum time as a PFC, exactly to the day, four months. From there I went and got a gamma globulin shot in the rear. My memory of how painful it was was unfortunately refreshed (two big Marines passed out cold in our platoon). Then we went to helicopter indoctrination, jumping in, flying up, jumping out. I always love flying in helos over the ocean and mountains. It's great. These were the big things, but a lot of little things happened also to make this a well-rounded but weird day.

Love,
DJE

PS Please address my letters as L/Cpl Eigen instead of PFC.

Deadly Meat Grinder

I was always goal-oriented. Obtaining rank is something I understood. I made Eagle Scout when I was thirteen and really loved going through the ranks. I was proud, but soon my ambitions were totally crushed as I got lost in the giant deadly meat grinder that was Vietnam.

Well, we finally landed and off-loaded in Okinawa and have been here about six days. This place is wonderful, beautiful, exotic, and full of pleasure. The barracks alone are great, better than any in the corps. In them we have partitioned rooms, wall and foot lockers, and comfortable racks. The main reason these quarters are the best is that our barracks have two house boys who shine shoes, clean, and do laundry. There are three [women] who do anything and another who will do all your sewing. Any of these services are extremely cheap. Our barracks only holds ninety-six people. For example, we had a very important inspection by the captain and I did nothing but pay a dollar fifty to have everything prepared. As for liberty, it is wonderful. There are many towns and many, many clubs. Cab fare clicks a nickel to your fifty cents. The base club, one of two, is second best to going to town. It has a floor show, twelve slot machines, serves beer and mixed drinks (beer is fifteen cents a bottle, mixed drinks twenty cent), a restaurant, and dancing with beautiful [young women].

Let me tell you about my liberty in town. The only reason I am not there now is because I am broke. But I have not yet believed that I am even off the ship, much less sitting in a beautiful bar with a beautiful [woman] on each arm. One thing I am sure Charles would like is that there is no age discrimination. All in all, I have had an unforgettable time and my only regret is that I do not have more money. I will write soon.

Daryl

PS Next stop, Philippine Islands.

The River Hades

We are now in the Philippines where we are awaiting a field problem. Last night I pulled liberty and was able to see the town. It is definitely "groovy." For example, right before you enter this limbo you have to cross the river of Hades. You accomplish this feat by tenderly picking your way over a scroungy bridge trying to disregard the calls & cackles from unknown creatures below. The stench is nauseating but the shouts pull you to the side where you linger and satisfy your curiosity by looking over and below. There they are, the children of the world standing on flimsy dugouts offering their bodies, while the others are screaming, shouting for coins. This seems quite romantic; however, the river is an open sewer with every toilet emptying directly into it.

I made it to town where I picked my way past deformities, disease, beggars, and smoking pots to keep malaria mosquitoes away. Finally, in the Western cultured areas I was able to have a very pleasurable time.

Daryl

Port of Call

The town was Olongapo, outside Subic Bay. It was raw. I remember that twice while I was there sailors turned up dead floating in the river. With a wad of cash I would go bouncing from one bar to the next. Sometimes I would go upstairs to get laid by a young Filipino [woman] with flashing neon lighting the bed. I was always worried about the banana gravity blade some of the women or the bouncer carried. A banana gravity blade came in many sizes from two inches to two feet. They were made from car leaf springs. Banana gravity blades had a unique design with a split handle that folded around the blade. With deftly trained hands the knife would emerge from a hidden place and one side of the handle would be thrown open and caught in the same hand exposing the blade.

I liked a four feet, eleven inch, brown-skinned young woman who everyone called "little potato." She had such a sweet smile.

Every night there would be a brawl between sailors and Marines. It was great fun to run from the shore patrol and hop a speeding "jeepney" decorated with silver bangles that cruised the main drag. One had to be careful to pay and leap off in time; otherwise they often would drive you beyond the town limits where muggers would wait to roll you. On the street we would eat strips of grilled meat, purported to be monkey, that were made by grungy street vendors. Every morning I would drag my sorry ass back to the Quonset hut in time for reveille. After several visits I became braver and ventured off the main street. I ran into some Americans who lived there. I was deeply intrigued with the possibility of living outside the states. I had heard they were deserters from somewhere. This played on my mind. I wondered how this could happen.

Stupid Questions and Lessons Learned
We had a series of jungle training classes and exercises. We were sitting in a jungle clearing listening to a Marine NCO give us a lecture using a green chalkboard. He said, "The only stupid question is the question not asked." A Marine up front immediately put up his hand. The lecturer called on him and he asked a question. The lecturer scratched his head and rubbed his chin. And then he said, "In all my years of giving courses, I never truly heard a stupid question until now. Son, that does not deserve an answer." He continued his lecture uninterrupted. I am sure that was his goal.

I was sitting there listening to him when something made me look at my shoulder. A huge tarantula was waiting to climb onto my ear. I took my hand and flicked him off my shoulder with one movement. I stood up and yelled, "Tarantula." All the Marines stood up. With me in the lead, we ran over the lecturer and the chalkboard. Class dismissed.

We boarded ship again to be ready to support an operation in Vietnam. It seems impossible but my memory is very clear on this experience. I was on deck leaning on the ship's railing as we pulled out of Subic Bay. It was raining in a couple of isolated spots. A rainbow appeared at the side of the ship. We were moving and turning. The end of the rainbow approached the ship. It was headed right for me. We intersected, and it disappeared and then appeared again on the other side of the ship. I felt blessed.

It's the Very Little Things that Count
USS Iwo Jima

Today I had a lesson in "it's the little things, the very little things that count." It is amazing how clean quarters with music plus a couple of sheets, a pillow and mattress, good chow, a personalized locker, and above all a cooperative navy crew can change the morale in a matter of hours. This came about when we transferred off the aircraft carrier USS Valley Forge by helicopter and on to the landing platform for helicopters for the USS Iwo Jima. On the Valley Forge I was sleeping on a bare piece of [canvas] with five other racks above me and was unable to turn over. There was just enough room to slide in sideways on either my back or stomach. Now I am sleeping in spacious quarters better than the staff NCOs because of the new ship and the fact of my odd job. I am eighty-one's (a high angle of fire weapon) forward observer radio operator attached from communications platoon to eighty-one mortars to Kilo company (3/26). I am so specialized and attached so many times nobody knows who I am. They have made me responsible to one man, my forward observer, who figures out where the rounds go and adjusts them. However, he just made staff and has to be billeted in staff quarters so nobody bothers me. When a field problem comes I just go out and do my job.

My spirits are so high. I have been here in Da Nang harbor for about two weeks. Believe me, at night Da Nang is a sight, watching the sky being continually lit up by flares and other devices. We have not yet seen action but have been committed for more than a month and can be called in at any time. But the chance is unlikely as we are soon heading back to the Philippines for some liberty and more training. In December we are going back in to set up a permanent camp for the rest of our tour. Even though we haven't gone in, we are still collecting combat pay for just being here.

(Two days later.)

Well, we have now been up and down the coast at least once, not including our night maneuvers. We are all standing by and are ready in case they start pushing at the DMZ. But I doubt that we will have the opportunity to go in. Everyone is restless and they are gnawing at the bit. I cannot deny that I feel the same way.

Yours, Daryl

The Marine Corps Birthday

Today is November 10, the 191st anniversary of the Marine Corps. We are pulling out of Vietnam today and going back to Okinawa, and then to the Philippines. We will be in the Philippines until December 5 and then we will be moving into Vietnam, probably for the rest of my tour.

Everything here is fine and with the strenuous exercises we maintain every day, I am getting in very good shape. I hope everything at home is well and running smoothly. Next week I'll be very busy changing ships.

Daryl

Good Liberty and Hard Training
11-22-66

Again we have moved. We are now in the SLF (Special Landing Force) camp in Subic Bay, Philippines, and we will be here for about a month. There is little to tell. We have good liberty but hard training. It seems I haven't stopped training since I joined the corps. The barracks we live in are brand new and are like the ones we had in boot camp. However, they are so new we have no racks or lockers and we must live out of sea bags and sleep on air mattresses. Fortunately, we are in the rainy season. I say fortunately because we will miss a lot of training that is only repetition anyway.

Ribbons

Finally they are cutting us some slack. I have been in PI (Philippines, their spelling) for about twelve days now and we pull liberty every night. I am now broke but we get paid tomorrow. Plus we earned combat pay when we were floating outside of Da Nang. We are still on twenty-four-hour standby, but I doubt if we will be called in.

Last night I went to the Sky Club, one of the enlisted men's clubs on the base. Like other nights they had performers from Australia, Hong Kong, Spain, France, and Japan. It was a very sophisticated show.

Yesterday, like many days, I went and got a haircut, shave, shampoo, massage, and tonic treatment for fifty cents; you can't beat that price anywhere.

I really do appreciate the packages that you send. If it is not too much trouble I would appreciate more packages with presweetened powdered drinks like Kool-Aid and small cans of food like sardines, nuts, homemade cookies, and fudge.

It is the monsoon season and it rains almost all the time, but it really doesn't bother me. I've always liked the rain anyway. Also, I now rate the Vietnamese ribbon and the new one that is coming out in March. I already have the National Defense ribbon and will probably rate a fourth ribbon for supporting the 3/3 in an operation in Vietnam. Although we didn't go in, we were the reactionary force. This will probably be just a few of the ribbons that we will rate before it is all over.

Daryl

A Hellish Place of Angels

> *A soldier will fight long and hard for a bit of colored ribbon.* —Napoleon

Rude Awakening

I am so nonchalant about going to Vietnam because I have such a romantic notion of war. I thought I was Ernest Hemingway until I found out he was an ambulance driver.

Toward the end of my stay I returned to the barracks about 3:00 a.m. I was drunk and alone. I was the only one who had enough money to take liberty. I had made some friends in town and was getting free drinks and other favors. When I came into the barracks I turned on the light and disturbed everyone. Suddenly the lights went out and I felt pain in my face. I woke up the next day and everyone had gone to maneuvers. There was dried blood all over. It was my blood. Someone had smacked me with a board.

I went to sick bay where they set my nose and said it was too late for stitches. The inside of my lip was torn open. I was more worried I was estranged from the unit and we were about to go into combat. I couldn't help thinking it was because of my being a Jew. Or maybe they were sick of my disturbing their sleep every night.

Later that day when the group got back I demanded to know who the coward was who hit me in the dark. I realized I had no friends and stood there looking at all of them ready to fight. One guy stepped forward and we began to struggle. It was soon broken up but there was a bad feeling. I felt alone. I was also scared. I was sure I would need all of them to survive in Vietnam.

The Next Day Comes, No Matter What
12-8-66
USS Lenawee

Again I find myself aboard ship. It's as if I've never been on land. I must say I had a great time in PI. We should be aboard this ship for about four days, where we will then make an administrative landing in Vietnam. This will finish our tour as the Special Landing Force for the Seventh Pacific Fleet. We will then proceed to Dong Ha, about twelve miles inland and about ten miles from the DMZ, in War Zone A or rather, the I corps. The ship we are presently on is the USS Lenawee.

I've made some good purchases in Okinawa: a 35 mm Cannon, and in the Philippines, a pair of prescription sunglasses and a scuba diving watch. When I return I plan to buy something for everyone at home. Right about now Christmas should be in the air but a hot jungle or a metal ship is not very conducive to a Christmas spirit. I am afraid when a Christmas carol comes over the air on the radio it is more than slightly out of shape.

Also, I tend to lose my bearings along the time element, not only from hour to hour or day to day but usually week to week. This is because time is really unimportant. The next day will come no matter what one does. I think only about this minute. If I don't do this, I find myself doing something worse and that is living in the future, when I get home. By living in the moment I can have fun without worrying about that inspection, hike, or what have you.

Daryl

PS When is Hanukkah?

Staying In Line

On board the *Lenawee* we essentially just stood in line for breakfast, lunch, and dinner. It was the same line. When I finished breakfast I would go to the end of the line and wait for lunch. There wasn't much else to do. The racks were in the hold and stacked up one on top of another. The guy above me was huge. The canvas stretched down under his weight and practically touched my nose.

When the seas got rough people would start puking. The stench was unbearable. I tried to sleep topside.

One of the guys couldn't sleep below either, and he always slept soundly with his eyes open. One morning he slept late on deck on his back. He had hard abs like any Marine but only above his belt. Below his belt was a funny paunch. On top of it all, above his chin was a very crooked smile. A crowd gathered around him thinking he had fallen from the rigging and was dead. I moved through the crowd and gave him a nudge with my foot. His subsequent movement startled everyone and made us laugh. Soon enough he and others would be lying on their backs with their eyes wide open, not moving and not laughing.

Part III

The 'Nam

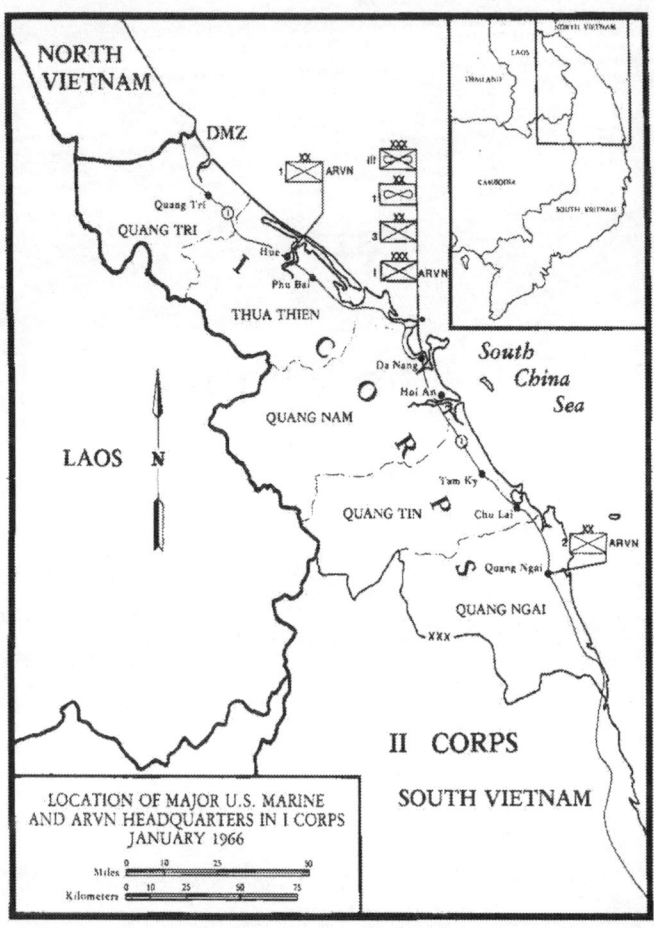

South Vietnam I Corps Map

Hitting the Beach
12-11-66
USS Lenawee

Tomorrow we hit the beach and move inland. Here in the ship's compartment there are many mixed feelings. Some of the guys are introspective, others are furiously sending their "last" letters, others are afraid, and some are overly normal. As for myself, I feel the same way I did yesterday and the many days before. This is not bravery. Tomorrow is only supposed to be an administrative landing with minimal ammo.

Daryl

A Movie Landing

On December 12, 1966, the Special Landing Force (SLF) for I Corps 3/26 landed at the mouth of a river at Dong Ha. The landing was right out of the movies. We climbed down the side of the ship with a full set of gear on large square rope nets into bouncing landing craft. The seas were turbulent and dangerous. I was acutely aware if I got into the wrong place the boat could pull away and come crashing back, crushing me between the landing craft and the ship, or, at the very least knock me into the ocean with eighty pounds or more of gear strapped to my back. I would be quickly dragged under. I waited, gauging the rhythm of the seas before I entered the craft. After successfully arriving, I then chipped in by holding the net.

I was in one of the first landing craft. I had to stand crowded among my mates. The sides of the craft were high to protect us from the seas and enemy fire. The seas were getting rougher. Things started to go bad and we circled and circled. People started to barf and wretch.

That morning we had had navy beans for breakfast. Out of the corner of my eye there was something rolling back and forth in time with the pitching of the ship, coming in view a little clearer each time. I soon realized the mess was the breakfast beans hardly digested at all. Swallowed whole. I was already nauseous from the fear, the smell of vomit, and the rolling of the ship. I started puking. I puked until it hurt and then dry-heaved some more. The heat of the sun made me weak. Sweat soaked my shirt, and my face was clammy. We circled and circled and together we heaved.

We finally came ashore and the ramp went down onto the sandy beach. We were the first to land, and grateful at that. If there had been any resistance it would have been deadly. We quickly hit the ground, loving the firmness and solidity of the earth. After doing the low crawl up the beach to check for the enemy, we were told to fall in. We lined up and were issued more ammo.

Sandbagged Bunkers
12-15-66

Well, I am finally here. We're set in at a mouth of a river, right next to an ocean, the South China Sea. We live in sand-bag bunkers and I managed to acquire a home that is the envy of all, including my section leader. Last night we sent out patrols and one was ambushed. No one got hurt and they suspect one VC kill. This morning I and about thirty more went out in armed amtracs (amphibious tracked vehicles) sweeping the area. We found where they had dragged the body.

Otherwise things are pretty decent. We eat C-rations but I like them better than hot chow. The mortars fired illumination all night.

    Daryl

On the Beach
I will never forget the nights by the beach with the moon lighting up the area like it was a spotlight. The bay gleamed and glistened. The sand shined and the bunkers cast shadows. It was so surreal with flares bringing flashes of color against the black sky. My mind and vision were keen and everything had more life. I was never more alive and clear than those first few months in Vietnam.

    Later the numbness would cover my heart like a dense shroud.

Tan All Over
12-20-66

As funny as it may seem, today I went sunbathing and swimming at the beach, which happens to be our front yard. Although I had to avoid concertina wire and was weighted down by my rifle, I still managed to get a tan (all over). Tonight we get a ration of cold beer, two cans that I am looking forward to. Tomorrow we are moving out and going farther south, like around Phu Bai, but I'll write more about this later. Yesterday evening a patrol from J Company was hit by VC mortars. Two were killed and five wounded. The day before this, on a sweep that I was on, we managed three casualties, all of which rate purple hearts.

Well, things are really pretty easy over here but we lack one thing and that is cigarettes. I hate to keep asking things of you, but I wish you would send out a few cartons of Pall Malls. Also, for the hard times, I wish you could send along a fifth of bourbon whiskey. We are allowed this and actually rate a liquor ration, but we haven't been able to receive this, nor will we be able to in the near future. So this bottle of whiskey and those few packages of cigarettes will be more than appreciated.

I'll write soon.

Daryl

The Promise of Death

I learned to smoke cigarettes in the rain, in the wind, and at night so the enemy couldn't see the flame or the glow of the ember. I could suck a wet cigarette, pulling the smoke through the water like a hookah. Later when I was farther in the bush, sundry packs were dropped by air transport. The boxes would drift down on black parachutes filled with cigarettes and candy. We patiently waited for our treasures with our necks crunched back and our hands shielding our eyes from the sun.

The promise of death at every turn brings one to the moment like nothing else. In the beginning when death is fresh everything tastes wonderful. Cigarettes are especially good at this time as they remind us of our power over fire and our willingness to play with death.

My family never understood that I was already sufficiently aged by circumstances. But rather they were in serious denial and thought my requests for cigarettes and liquor frivolous.

Foxhole
12-22-66

I really don't know what to say. I am sitting in my foxhole on radio watch. We take turns listening to the radio on selected frequencies as well as guarding the perimeter. Just about thirty minutes ago I came in off a patrol. We caught a few sniper rounds from a hut so we mortared it to the ground. Last night our lines were hit and we suffered minor casualties. VC suffered fifty-eight confirmed killed and three captured. I am not so sure you want to hear this, but I can't see lying to you.

I am really quite healthy and happy and I doubt that I'll have much trouble while I am here. The letters will now become quite scarce because we are going on a sweep. We are now set in just below Phu Bai and the terrain looks like our Kettle Moraine. Actually, they are the foothills before the mountains. It really doesn't seem like four days until Christmas, especially in one hundred-plus degree heat and me with sunglasses and a beautiful tan.

    Daryl

Dig Deep, Wide, and Continuous
I learned to dig deep, wide, and continuously. Wherever we would go I would dig a hole. Whenever we would stop even for a brief

A Hellish Place of Angels

moment I would start digging. Sometimes I would have to remove the grass first before I could dig. Other times the earth was bare. In the jungle the earth was loamy, dark, and fertile. I was a farmer digging for life. I would plant myself in the hole just dug to sprout the next day with the morning sun.

I'd made up my mind I would always be working on a hole. My E-tool (folding shovel) became as much my friend as my rifle. The E in E-tool stood for entrenchment. It has a short handle and a slightly concave shovel face that comes to a point. The shovel has three useful positions: the face folds over the handle and locks in the folded position; the face at ninety-degrees perpendicular to the handle; and fully deployed with the face in line with the handle. A sleeve screw locks the shovel face in whichever position is chosen. I learned to use the E-tool as a seat when I had to make a contribution to nature and I devised ways to use it for hand-to-hand combat.

Foxholes probably went more toward saving my life than anything else. I would first dig a foxhole like a coffin, one I could lie down in. This was the easiest because the topsoil was looser than the subsoil. At night I would lie horizontal in my first-stage hole.

In the beginning I had an air mattress, which, when put into a new hole, had me above ground. Once we came under fire while I was in this position. The plan was to take out my bayonet and stab the air mattress and then fix the air mattress in the morning. However, when the shit hit the fan I stabbed it many times more than planned. And that was the end of my air mattress.

Later in my tour my foxholes became more sophisticated. I started to get paranoid and fantasize about the use of nuclear weapons. After all, we were fighting a surrogate war with China and the Soviet Union. I remembered the training films we had seen, but more importantly I remembered my father's responsibilities as a regional radiation control officer for the civil defense. On our coffee table was a book titled *Blast Radius and Fallout Statistics*. In our basement was a sizable Geiger counter complete with radioactive samples. Judging by my father's interest, it was only a matter of time before we were in a nuclear war.

I crouched in my foxhole and remembered crouching in a hallway during a grade school emergency nuclear disaster drill. I always imagined the bomb falling during these drills and the plentiful glass shattering, raining shards across all of us frightened children.

I dug foxholes on sweeps. Most did not. A sweep involved one or more battalions to move through an area looking for VC. The battalion would position its companies to cover a wide area but in such a way as to mutually protect each other. Often the terrain would force the sweep to resolve itself into a column of one size or another, sometimes with flanking elements. It always involved movement. Digging a foxhole really involved starting many holes and finishing only a few. We never knew where we were going or when we would stop. Day after day, sometimes for months, we would be in the bush, walking and looking for the enemy. It was like a game of Go. (The game of go is an ancient Chinese board game for two players that emulates some strategic actions of war such as enveloping the enemy while being ambushed.) We would encircle to ambush and so would they. It was hard to tell who was winning. Every night we would stop and dig in. Then we might move again to confuse the enemy, or move and set up an ambush. Wherever we went I would dig another hole, no matter how tired I was from marching and digging.

Short Round
12-25-66

Dear Family,

Well, we were hit again last night and have been receiving mortar rounds all day. In the five days we have been here we have killed more than one hundred fifty VC and captured a few. We have suffered two killed in action and about fifty wounded in action.

It rains all the time, but my foxhole is set up with drains and trenches and sandbags so I manage to stay dry. The reason this letter is such a mess is because I am writing between calling in mortar rounds. I am part of a two-man forward observing team. I carry a radio and my sergeant, the other member of the team, carries the map case and computes. I am the assistant FO. He and I go out with the company (Kilo) and set up night defensive fire plans and fire when our lines are hit. The 81s down in the command post got hit last night and the night before by incoming mortar rounds. Nineteen of my friends were wounded and two guns out of eight were put out of action.

Today a 60 mm mortar, which is the one the companies carry, was registering its rounds and they had a short round, which killed two Marines in our perimeter. They do not rate forward observers so they have to fire by direct lay. But it really was nobody's fault, just bad ammo.

Daryl

Tableau of Horror

I remember hearing the round go off and saw that it had been fired over the bulk of the main force. The troops were strewn over a wide area down the side of a hill. I remember thinking, *It was a bad idea to fire over the company position.* I saw the round go up and wondered, *Why could I see it, and why was it so slow?* The round did not go far and landed in a foxhole below me. I saw the two Marines blown from their hole. In a way it was fortunate it landed in the hole or more would have been killed. The odd thing is hardly anyone blinked at the tableau of horror before them.

When a mortar round explodes it makes a "whump" sound. Shrapnel makes a buzzing sound. Given the blast angle, it is safest to get down or into the ground as fast as possible. I became adept at hitting the deck at lightning speed even without a hole.

Daryl J. Eigen

Funeral Procession
12-27-66

Dear Family,
    You might not believe it, but it has rained for eight continuous days now with no sign of letup. It is also astonishingly cold. It is probably forty-five degrees with the wet rain and cold wind. Yesterday we went on a combat patrol. The rice paddies in the valleys are flooded. While crossing one we received sniper fire. Because the water was over our heads we could not get across in time to get them. While coming back we lost a man. He was not shot but drowned because of the high water. The patrol turned into a funeral procession when we finally recovered his body.
    I have grown a mustache and I look quite decent. I might even keep it.
    I received Aunt Jean and Uncle Izzie's money order and am very grateful. Please show them this letter. For the reasons mentioned in the preceding paragraph I lost it. I hope they kept the stub to that money order. With a radio, rifle, helmet, cartridge belt, ammo, grenades, and flak jacket, I had to swim across the raging stream. I was more worried about getting across than saving that money order. Anyway, I really have no use for money or stamps here. So please cash the stub and bank it. I will probably be sending more money to save for my education. I also have a fifty-dollar monthly allotment that collects 10 percent interest.
    Is Donna going back to college? Is Chuck doing all right in school? I hope everything is well and I'll write as soon as possible. C'est la guerre!
    Daryl

PS Tell Kita I appreciated her card.
Note: Kita was our dog.

Harsh Judgment

While camping on the other side of the river we were ordered by the captain to shave. Everyone was angry to get such a spit-and-polish directive when we were in combat. I had to shave with my K-bar combat knife in the river as I bathed. I left the mustache.

The captain was tall and blond, wore a white scarf, and carried a swagger stick. He was quite taken with his swashbuckling self. Later, he, with part of his Company, was caught by surprise by a sniper in a small river boat. I was not there, but the word was he only had holes in his back from his own troops. At the time it seemed just. I guess we had a low tolerance for bullshit.

Later on I would hear more rumors of fragging (killing superior officers who were assholes or gung ho with a fragmentation grenade). Grenades left little ballistics or direction of fire. At least it afforded them a purple heart if done during battle.

Xmas Cease Fire

Dear Folks,

Well, today is Christmas Eve and I received that Seasons Greetings card with the two pictures of Chuck and Dad and Sam. The letter made me feel very good. Today is also the beginning of the cease fire standoff. It started at 7:00 a.m. and we fought right up till then. It is calm at least for the time being. It seems we are the only hot spot in Vietnam. The newsmen and cameras (CBS) are in the battalion CP (command post) and are interviewing the men because we have taken 154 confirmed dead VC, a possible 300 dead VC, and double this [in] wounded and about 20 captured in the week and a half we have been here. This started out to be an operation but now we are digging in and moving in more companies. It seems we have run into a regiment of VC trying to harvest the rice.

Today I went down to the guns (81s) and they're doing a damn fine job. Almost every fourth man is wounded and they are still running the guns. As for myself, I am unharmed and see no reason to change; except for being slightly wet I am very content.

I seem to fit right into this war and fighting comes second hand. I suppose I sound "salty" as hell but I am here, I've been through it, and, I must say, I am none the worse.

Season's Greetings, Happy Hanukkah, and Happy New Year.

Daryl

PS We should be in the news, both paper and TV. Look for Battalion Three, Regiment Twenty-Six, Fifth Division, Marines, Kilo Company in I Corps area thirty-five kilometers from Phu Bai.

The Thrill of Staying Alive

There was a small innocuous paragraph that was part of a front page story in the *New York Times* that acknowledged this ceasefire violation (New York Times, 1966). It wasn't a declared war, so a declared ceasefire did not mean very much.

I started to get good at what I was doing. I liked being in combat. It was thrilling to be competent at staying alive.

Free Killing Zone

1-13-67

I will tell you what I do each day. Every morning I get up at the crack of dawn, get my radio, pick up my FO (Forward Observer), and go to an observation point where we call in fire and level villages and people who are running around. We are in a free killing zone where any person we see is either VC or sympathizers. Every once in a while, [we] air-drop free conduct passes and warnings for the [indigenous population] to get out of the area. Then we get a combat patrol ready and sweep the area, find and scoff up all the people (shoot if they run), turn them over to the army of the Republic

A Hellish Place of Angels

of Vietnam, and count confirmed dead. The only problem is we sometimes receive sniper fire and always run into booby traps and punji pits. (Punji pits are camouflaged pits with the bottom covered with sharpened feces-covered bamboo sticks that would pierce your torso if you fell into it. If that didn't kill you maybe the infection caused by the toxic shit would.) But since I am in the command post group, I walk along a checked route and am fairly well covered. We then come back and fire into the area again and then send out night ambushes and listening posts. I get a few days off alternating with artillery FOs.

We were pulled out of our original positions to go on a three-company sweep, about five grid squares from the battalion area (five thousand meters). We have made the news. I have already seen some of the clippings. This operation is called Operation Chinook. We are located about forty-five kilometers north of Phu Bai and about forty kilometers south of Dong Ha. Both of these [bases have] air strips.

Phu Bai, Da Nang, and Chu Lai can be found on a big map along the coast, and south of the DMZ is the I Corps area. I am sure you have heard of Da Nang!

The mouth of the river where we hit the beach and stayed a week received VT (variable time fuse) mortars from the enemy, and the Marines sustained 44 percent casualties and four dead. Also, Dong Ha got hit the next night. This was only twenty-four hours after we had vacated the area. Of course we get casualties every day, if not from VC then from our own carelessness. Yesterday a guy playing with a grenade in a tent blew up himself, the tent, and eleven other people. Accidental discharges and short rounds occur much too frequently.

The weather here is like nothing you have heard. It is very similar to Korea during certain seasons and much like our late fall. It has rained twenty days without letting up and it is cold! About forty-five degrees at night and no more than sixty degrees in the daytime, and with jungle gear that's (((cold))). I am so used to rain that it really doesn't bother me any more, and they now have a warm-up tent where we can dry off and get warm. Soon, in a couple of months, we will be sweating in one hundred-twenty-degree heat wishing for rain and cool weather.

Right now we are operating in the hill country and lowlands. I guess they are planning to move up to the mountains. As far as disease goes, dysentery is universal, and immersion foot (trench foot) and hyperhidrosis (excessive sweating) have claimed about 95 percent of this battalion's roll call. As for myself, I am just like everyone else. We try to keep clean shaven and washed up but nobody has taken a full shower for about three weeks. All we eat is C-rations and supplements, which consist of candy and cigarettes. Sometimes we get hot soup, fresh bread, and ham. I am just telling you the facts, which probably sound much worse than we take them. Believe me, we have more than grown used to the situation.

  Daryl

Never So Cold

The coldest I have ever been was in Vietnam. One night it was raining and we came under fire. The battle grew worse, as did the monsoons. Eventually I could not get out of my foxhole because we were taking so much fire. The ground became a shiny field of gray mud reflecting the light from the flares.

A small stream started and quickly filled up my foxhole. There was cold rainwater and mud washing through my hole up to my neck, carrying away my body heat. That night I was so cold I just softly cried all night. By the morning I was shaky and disoriented. My skin and lips were gray, numb, and wrinkled. Hypothermia is sneaky. If I had known more I would have been scared.

A Hellish Place of Angels

Battalion Aid Station

PHU BAI—"In addition to holding routine sick call for the unit, the primary function of this Battalion Aid Station is to treat and hold here as many minor cases as possible," said navy lieutenant Jim C. Nauman.

'Since we arrived at this position Dec. 19, it's rained steadily except for about four days," said Chief Hospital man H. D. Starr.

"As a result, there has been a tremendous number of cases of immersion foot, skin boils, and other skin infections," the chief corpsman said. ("Battalion Aid Station," Sea Tiger, January, 1967.)

The article went on to say that of the fifty-two navy personnel assigned to the battalion, twenty were doctors and thirty-two were field corpsmen of whom about twenty had been awarded purple hearts for battlefield wounds.

Moldy Salami
1-20-67

Yesterday I received your package dated January 3 and it was the thirteenth. That's awfully fast. Today I received a package dated November 21. Yesterday's package contained everything I needed: gum, foot powder, wash towels (that's the first chance I have had to get clean in a month, or at least halfway clean), and cigarettes. This package was perfect. Today's package was another surprise, for it has goodies that sure hit the spot. But the two salamis were moldy (when I felt the package I knew what they were), so you can understand how disappointed I was when I broke them out. I tried to eat them anyway but didn't succeed. I hope you realize what a morale booster these packages and your letters give me and I thank you very much.

Today, however, was not a happy day. It still has not stopped raining (more than twenty-five days without sunshine) and besides sniper rounds, we received eleven casualties and one dead. A reactionary force from our company went out to investigate an outpost under fire and someone tripped a booby trap. The day before yesterday I was involved in a firefight with this same platoon. My FO and I called in mortar rounds and I got a chance to fire my 45. One man, a machine gunner, was wounded. I own, or rather possess, an automatic M14, but I find with a radio that a 45 is a lot easier to handle. But I'll tell you, when the shit hits the fan like it did then and you see bullets hitting the dust and people yelling, "Corpsman," I wished I had my rifle. But I came out unharmed. I called in the air medevac for the injured man via air observers and a fixed winged Piper Cub. I was complimented for doing an outstanding job because we were under fire and it was a complex procedure by the platoon commander who, by the way, was one of the ones wounded today. All in all I am relatively safe because I am part of the CP (command post) and am surrounded by grunts, who trip all the mines before I get there.

Daryl

PS If you send sausage again, send it air mail and wrap it in tin foil.

Too Much Mail

I remember getting those packages in the field. One was filled with cookie dust, which everyone ate, and the other had those moldy sausages. We were in high grass sporadically engaged with the enemy.

A Hellish Place of Angels

We had been choppered in and were surprised to get mail call with the medevacs. The mail bags were unloaded and the wounded, with bloody gauze trailing, took their place. I received more mail than all the rest of the unit combined. It consisted of several brightly colored nylon bags filled with mail. I was very excited about getting so much, even though the situation made it hazardous to be so encumbered. I thought, *How can I carry it all?* We were not going to stay long enough to even dig a very big hole.

Besides the single gift box, the mailbags were filled with old, soaked *Chicago Tribunes*. Someone had chosen my name for a free subscription as part of a campaign to support the troops. We were deep in the bush and on the move so I had to quickly bury the bags and papers. I was hunched over so I wouldn't make a very big target. I was laughing at the irony of it all, which took the edge off the extra work needed to bury the papers. The rest of the unit was totally baffled.

I had to run to catch the choppers that were transporting us to the next fight. The choppers swirled the colored smoke that marked the LZ (landing zone). The colored smoke reminded me of the colored mailbags I was leaving behind.

Testing the Bible
1-24-67

Well, we are still on Operation Chinook but my company is now within the battalion perimeter. All of this time we have been operating outside of the perimeter as more or less the assault force. I have been pulled back to 81s as a section operator for a little rest. Being a forward observer is trying, to say the least, especially when humping a radio. This rain here is really quite unexplainable. Hell, thirty days in a row seems to be testing the Bible. And I never cease to be amazed how much different the temperature is from what I heard before I arrived. But I am hardly the misinformed one. For the day before yesterday, I received a portable fan from Barb and Barry. It was marvelous hearing from them but I was standing near a fire trying to get warm and that fan more or less shows how little the people back home know about where we are. I'll tell you, it is as cold here as it is in November where you are. But it's only the monsoon season, and soon I will be more than thankful for the fan and the weather will conform to everyone's thinking and the sun will shine.

Maybe you, Mom, will be interested to know that they have come up with something to stop immersion foot, an ailment that has been taking a high cost of men during all this rain. It is a sticky gelatin, mostly silica, that you spread on your feet to waterproof them. With this, plus jungle boots, they say you can't catch it.

We still get action from the VC but only in the form of snipers, booby traps, mortars, and hit and run. They manage to get a few good men and it is frustrating as hell to receive fire and not to be able to see anyone, or to get wounded and dead and get no enemy in return. However, if you remember or possibly read in the paper, we were at the beginning aggressed by a regiment of hard-core VC in a series of banzai, human wave attacks, as the paper put it. We survived with a few casualties and no dead but took 175 enemy casualties. There were countless more, but the VC have a bad habit of dragging their bodies away. In fact, when the illumination goes up, you can see their working parties dragging, you shoot, and the illumination goes out. When it comes up, everyone is gone, including the draggers you shot. You see, every fourth man in a VC outfit is a dragger and all he carries is a grabbing hook with a long rope. They dispose of the bodies in nearby villages. The next day, when we make a sweep, we find fresh graves.

Twice on New Year's Day the battalion was the first to violate the ceasefire. This made the news because we were being attacked again by hardcores in excess of one thousand troops. Recon spotted them early and artillery let them have it. Recon reported direct hits and it stopped the battalion from being hit. This brought our total kills for this operation up to six hundred, quite a good number for the green battalion we are, or let's say were.

I read one clipping that said this battalion should have ceased to exist considering all that we have been hit with and right now is only here by a miracle. But [there is] no need to be alarmed. Most of it hardly seems like there is a war on. You also might be interested to know that we now have a new battalion commander, a new XO [executive officer], and a new H & S CO commander. Today the new colonel came around to 81s and introduced himself personally to each man and asked him questions and shook our hands. This is extremely rare for a Marine Corps colonel. But he seems like a good head and he was also congratulating us for the job we (81s) did during that big battle. He is trying to get 81s a citation or at least a letter of commendation in each of our record books.

 Daryl

Mortar Fights

Whenever we fired our 81 mortars the flashes could be spotted by the enemy. They would home in on our mortar flashes with their mortars. We would do the same and thus engage in a swap of mortars.

 Most often I was attached to an infantry company as a member of the FO team. I would see the mortar flashes and call in a response. Occasionally I was with the mortar unit and took my licks with them. It was wild trying to fire the mortars while there was incoming. Stand up, grab a round, take off the number of charges called for by the tables and let the round slide down the tube. Then crouch down until the outgoing round clears. If there was incoming, I would stay down until it was over, then fire the next rounds as ordered.

Sometimes it would get very confusing. It would seem like the rounds we were firing would be falling on us.

"Chinook Will Be Remembered for VC and Monsoon Rains"

By Sgt. Roger Ynostroza

PHU BAI—Marines stood huddled around a bonfire. Someone said he thought this must be what it's like on the moon—or anywhere your front practically burns—and your backside freezes. Facing the fire clad in water-logged flak jackets, jungle utilities, helmets and ponchos, "L" Company, Twenty-Sixth Regiment Marines braced themselves against the bitter-cold wind." (Ynostroza, "Chinook Will Be Remembered for VC and Monsoon Rains, *Sea Tiger,* March, 1967)

Once in the rear, when knowledge of our position was not a factor, we had a bonfire using wooden ammo boxes. We had been ringing wet for days with the rain coming down in sheets from black, cloudy skies. The wind was the worst, whistling through our meager shelters. There was not a lot of Christmas spirit, although the hot chow and supplies that were on the way helped some.

Our accommodations hardly rose to the level of shelter, as they only consisted of foxholes, ponchos, bamboo poles, and some line. They did little to help thwart the merciless rain and wind from making us miserable. Foxholes were equal parts mud and water. Nothing was dry.

Later that day we were resupplied with C-rats and ammo. Fresh bread and butter, bologna, oranges, and more wood were dispensed. Everything was piecemeal, but it was the best meal in a long time. Then came hot onion soup and hot coffee. It definitely made me feel better for the moment.

A Hellish Place of Angels

Ham and Mother Fuckers

I got so sick of eating C-rations and carrying them with me that I only selected and traded for ham and lima beans or ham and mother fuckers as we affectionately called them. The lima beans did not deserve the moniker of fuckers for the digestive issues they allegedly wrought. Rather it was probably the ham fat coagulated on top of the can. Since it was always easy to trade maybe everyone else just hated lima beans, hence the fuckers label.

I also carried a stick of C4 plastic explosive. Plastic explosive has the property of burning very fast and very hot without necessarily exploding unless dramatically disturbed, such as with a blasting cap. Every day in the field at some lull in the fighting or marching I would open a can of ham and MFs with the John Wayne can opener I wore with my dog tags around my neck. I would then break off a piece of plastic explosive and place it under the can. The explosive would burn in seconds and leave the can red hot with the lima beans and fat bubbling. I ate the chow quickly, often burning my mouth, so I would be ready to fight or duck. As the war wore on, I lost my appetite and was only eating one can a day. This helped, as we often were not supplied in a timely basis. I also had a bottle of hot sauce, which made all the difference. Occasionally I would have an onion.

Supply was erratic. Once we called in a medevac but they dropped C-rats and jerry cans of water from about forty feet from the helicopter. They landed on the wounded, killing one and further injuring another. How ignominious to be killed by flying C-rations.

A Friendly Lovers' Moon
2-1-67

Life goes fairly well now that I am back with the platoon. At least I have a fairly stable routine. That's something, anyhow. We have fashioned some ingenious bunkers that raise our living standards enough to satisfy a misguided social worker. And for the first time we have had two days of consecutive sun. Old sol is drying out the place with astonishing speed. There is even a slight hope that this is the break in the monsoon season. However, most probably I will be begging for rain, but, at least for now I have had enough.

Last night "The Moon Came over the Mountains" just like Kate Smith always promised, and it was a beautiful sight. It got so bright you could read a book. It was a complete full moon, the kind where you can see the craters and seas by the naked eye. However, it was not a wolf-howling moon, just a friendly lovers' moon.

But I am afraid the enemy also liked it because they attempted to pull movements to hit our lines. But we spotted them and cremated them with our guns, 81s, and artillery, scoring quite a few kills. So it was a good night, but just for our side.

No Longer Green
2-6-67

Dear Family,

Things are going really well and I find myself with plenty of free time. It hardly seems as if there is a war anymore. We are the first battalion in a long time to come into a new area in Vietnam, neutralize resistance, and proceed to build up the area. I remember when we first assaulted this area, nothing but hills, grass, valleys, and rice paddies. We were met with low resistance but the convoy hit many mines, inflicting many casualties. After settling in, we awaited nightfall, digging in as fast as possible. We had heard that several other battalions had tried to take this area but had been kicked out.

Seeing as how we were a comparatively green battalion (only one-and-a-half weeks at the mouth of the river with light action), we awaited the test. It came early in the morning when the VC frantically tried to overrun us with a series of human wave attacks. We crushed them, seemingly too easily. The next night they hit us with even greater ferocity. Again we checked them and repeated this for the next two nights.

Badly beaten, the Viet Cong pulled back to the mountains and we established ourselves.... We were no longer a "green" battalion. Now, two months later, the place looks like a small city with bunkers and tents. This area now will be destined to be as big as Phu Bai or Dong Ha and possibly bigger. We are assured of our position and are now operating out of this area at the base of the mountains. Possibly soon they will also put in an airstrip and another battalion will move in as Chinook II, but it will always be remembered that 3/26 was Chinook I and took this area with surprising swiftness.

Even now the bombers, artillery, and our own 81s are continuously bombing the surrounding terrain hoping to drive out the last diehard guerillas who remain in caves and holes. But this is not the finish because we will soon have to move to the mountains where the hardcores are; this, indeed, will be difficult but I am confident we will succeed.

Daryl

3/26 Pride

I was very proud of my battalion. 3/26 would later play an instrumental role in the siege of Khe Sanh in 1968.

Rough Rider
2-7-67

Today I went on the Rough Rider to Phu Bai, a supply run in a truck convoy. I was riding shotgun and was the forward observer. The trip takes approximately two hours, traveling south along Highway

1. The road is paved and is two-laned; however, the bridges were all blown out by terrorists and Cong and have been replaced by provisional steel barges. [That] makes it a rough trip. We passed through Hue, one of the bigger towns in this province, Quang Tri, and surprisingly enough it had all the earmarks of a modern town. With apartment houses, it looks like it was built in about the early fifties, and with grass, paved roads, and with smartly dressed businessmen going to work on Hondas, it seems out of place and definitely not a city in a war-torn country. Only our armed convoy marred this peaceful suburb.

Also, when riding through these villages and towns, one has the feeling of being much like the soldiers in WWII in France, riding through the streets with children by the droves and people screaming and waving. I felt like the liberator. But when we stopped to check for mines, my illusion was shattered, for the kids ran to the truck and their yells turned to pleas for food and cigarettes.

In Phu Bai I had my first hot meal of real food. I even had it on a plate! It's been about two months now.

Coming back again through the city of Hue, I thought of the many times I had walked through villages made of straw and mud, and I was amazed at the difference of living conditions between the city people of Hue and the backward farmers not many meters away.

Daryl

Convoy Driving Pretty Rough

PHU BAI—"When I pass the signpost, I know it's time to keep an extra sharp lookout. We're in VC territory now," he said. Lance Corporal Steven Laeno ... knows the exact time it will take to cover the twenty-five miles from Phu Bai to the Chinook command post, every village and landmark along the way, and most of the bumps. It is a monotonous ride; a series of stop and starts over deeply rutted roads of mud in the monsoon season, and hidden by clouds of dust in the summer. ("Convoy Driving Pretty Rough," *Sea Tiger*, January, 1967)

VC mined the road and sniped at the convoy on a daily basis.

Weird and Ugly

Kids would later become a hazard to convoys by throwing grenades into the trucks. In a senseless act of retaliation, a Marine I had never met heated up a can of food and tossed it to an unsuspecting kid. The kid was burned when he caught it and let loose with a string of profanity. I asked him what the fuck he was doing. He smiled a crazy grin. It was getting weird and ugly.

The September 30, 1967, edition of the *New Yorker* published a poem written on a flak jacket of a Marine corporal, Edward Broderick, who was on convoy on the road to Con Thien:

> When youth was a soldier and I fought across the sea
> We were young and cold hearts of bloody savagery.
> Born of indignation, children of our times. We were orphans of creation and dying in our prime.

Young Roses in a Camp of Thorns
2-10-67

Things are going very well. I am still here with the platoon and will probably stay for a few more weeks. I was awaiting transportation to take my place again as forward observer radio operator when my counterpart, the man who relieves me so I can take a couple of weeks out, was wounded by a bullet. But it turned out to be only a slight flesh wound and he volunteered to remain out so as to give me a little slack. This is my second relief. My first took sick. Also, this is his second Purple Heart. He received shrapnel in the hand when he was in the position I am in now. So, you see, I have been very lucky.

Every day we improve our bunkers. Ours is the best in 81s, and 81s are the best in the battalion. We have a squad-size bunker (only our squad is now down to seven). We have all the luxuries: wooden door, bunk beds, tables, wooden floor, lights, candles, and chairs. All built with my ingenuity and Marine Corps know-how.

Yesterday we received replacements for all the people who are no longer with us. Our platoon received seven, which wasn't enough, and our section got two of them, and my squad got one of the two. This is the picture: we were all standing around the gun, some of us working, some of us not, going through H & I (harassment and irritation) fire at known enemy positions. This day was no different from the rest or so it seemed. The staff sergeant (S. Sgt.), our section leader, came rather wobbly up to our guns, obviously slightly drunk, something I had never seen him do except on liberty in the Philippines. He yelled in a drunken voice for the section to muster around our gun. This consists of ten people. We all came close and awaited him. He looked at us with sad eyes and told us that he was glad to have us in the section and that we had all been through hell and back twice, and that we were the best section in the platoon (which is true).

After these heartwarming statements, [he gave] a confession that was truly sad but obviously [spurred on] by the liquor. He spoke of the time our section was attached with the line company Kilo. At the time I was the FO operator and we were on patrol. While searching a village, we were suddenly assaulted by automatic weapons and carbine fire. We engaged [the enemy and sustained] one seriously wounded [Marine]. They asked for support, so my FO and I called back to our section for fire. We got the adjusting rounds and called for a fire for effect. It never came. We continued to swap rounds with the VC, when my radio communications went out with the

A Hellish Place of Angels

section. I knew it wasn't my radio and I didn't understand what the problem was. Then, out of nowhere, two rounds seemingly landed in the center of our troops. I was in back of the platoon with the lieutenant to cover our rear and evacuate the wounded man. I finally got hold of the helo evacuation team and directed them in via my radio. We thought these rounds were incoming and checked for more casualties. But it turned out it was the rounds we had called for and they landed right on top of the VC, but they were so close that shrapnel was skimming over our heads. We never did find out the delay in those very important rounds till the S. Sgt. stood in front of us today and told us it was his fault and that he, for a moment, was scared; but he got his shit together and gave us those rounds.

We all sat looking at him, and he drunkenly looked back and then said we're getting two replacements tonight and we will hold an indoctrination lecture in his squad hut.

Later, we slowly, one by one, mustered in the bunker and awaited our new men. We all thought about the men these replacements were taking the place of, our friends and comrades since Las Pulgas, California. Their reasons for being gone were sad in each case. One was on emergency leave, his father was dying; another was transferred because he was strung like taut wire, ready to crack in an instant. We broke out some whiskey we had been saving and solemnly passed it around. Each dirty and unshaven face took a long, hard pull. Then the two new recruits were ushered in. They were alien! Their faces were awestruck and frozen in a look of shock. Like two young roses in a camp of thorns, they stuck out unbearably so. With brand new gear, clean faces, and black rifles with no rust while ours are silver from use.

Slowly, like robots, hunched down because of the low roof, they moved amongst us to the two places reserved for them. They awkwardly sat and remained silent with a look of two teenagers at an adult party. I felt old, like I had seen the world and was looking at the new generation. They were so young. The bottle of whiskey came around again and I drew another long slug and heard the S. Sgt. start his talk. He talked about the section and the fights we had been in, trying as hard as possible to give these guys the straight scoop so we wouldn't fill them with sea stories. But as he continued, their gaping mouths, if possible, got larger and their eyes grew wider.

Looking around, I saw my buddies and through the flickering candlelight I never felt closer. All of their faces said the same thing as mine as they stared at the strangers. We were veterans. We never really realized this before we were faced with these two outsiders. Also, we never realized how dirty we were. Sgt. kept on speaking, now introducing us, giving little friendly cracks about each one. We were all so close and these two lonely Marines wanted so much to be part of us. It was sad, but then again, it was good. The squad and section are working much better and the two [replacements] alleviates much of the strain. And, as always, when people are forced into a situation such as this one, they will eventually be incorporated. But as of now, they still sit out in the snow looking in the window at the fireplace.

Daryl

Incoming
2-14-67

Today is the beginning of the lunar holidays and the lunar truce. We will be firing illumination all night long for as long as the truce lasts. And considering the last two truces were repeatedly broken by both sides, we will not be lulled off guard. The night before last we received incoming mortars. They had our 81 position pinpointed and we were the only ones to receive any enemy fire. They shot fifteen rounds into our area, scoring five direct hits. Two (hit) on our supply tent, destroying chow and the tent, and three on our bunkers. All save one bunker held up. This bunker received a round directly in the center of its roof, collapsing it on top of its occupants, wounding two of the four inside by the sheer weight of the roof. We suffered two other casualties by shrapnel and considered ourselves lucky. The rounds stopped coming when we returned mortar fire. Almost every bunker has sandbags shredded and shrapnel lodged in various places. Also, all our vehicles were put out of action. The day before yesterday we got a new tent and a bulldozer came to help us dig in further. Yesterday evening we feared the worst, especially because we expected the VC to hit us before the holidays and truce. Everybody was a little nervous and we fired many missions of illumination and HE (high explosives) because the line company thought they saw VC. Two of the many missions we fired were valid, but we did score a few hits. Besides this, routine remains the same and the war goes on.

    Daryl

PS I received the package with the salami and rye bread ingeniously wrapped in paraffin and foil. For the first time since I have been in the corps, I had a real salami on rye sandwich and believe me, it tasted fresh from the store. The other items came in very handy and I really appreciated them. The only things I can ask for are cigars, cookies, and maybe some more salami (it went so fast) and fudge. I could go on because you have been brilliant in your selections of the things I need or want. I know it takes a lot of your time and efforts and I must compliment you and thank you.

Guernica

Sometimes there were bigger firefights or mortar exchanges, but more often at this time it was little skirmishes, booby traps, and light guerilla action. The heavy battles would come later against the North Vietnamese army (NVA).

Once we were firing our mortars at a tree line; there was someone running in the forest. We were some distance away on a ridge. The mortars started hitting and one person came running out of the forest. She had such an anguished look on her face. I can never forget. She was screaming and running. Her face and neck seemed to stretch toward us like a figure from a Chagall painting or Picasso's *Guernica*. Somehow I had the sense she wasn't mentally all there, although her terror was palpable. Everyone yelled, "Cease fire!" The rounds were already gone and the explosions overtook her.

Booby Traps

(Colette was a friend of my sister's who wrote me a few letters, saved them, and later returned them) Colette,

I received your letter,

 I am well aware of your fate in not having a direction as far as school goes and I know the frustration it undoubtedly causes. For a long time I floundered in the shallow waters that you are now entering, but I think I see a long, clear deep stretch ahead because, you see, my goals, drives, and objectives are at last becoming clear to me.

 As for Donna, she will soon come around, for she is possessed, as am I, with an urge to travel. This compulsion is probably the best explanation of my present situation and my future plans.

 Soon I'll be making a trip to Japan (Tokyo) on R&R, which will complete my tour of the Far East. In September when my combat tour has ended, I think I will extend six months and take advantage of a thirty-day gratis leave, which offers a free round-trip ticket to anywhere in the world. I will choose Europe, which you know I have always wanted to see. I am still undecided: my life, the price I would have to stake, is pretty expensive collateral and it will take some consideration.

A Hellish Place of Angels

I have just come in from an operation today. We at last managed to cross "the river" (a barrier that until now has enabled the Viet Cong and hardcores to snipe and mortar our positions). With tanks, Ontos (an armored track vehicle with 6 106mm recoilless rifles mounted on top), and my 81s, we set up on a ridge line overlooking the valley and the river. Directly across from us loomed the mountains, leaving the two sides of the trap open. Blocking up one end with artillery fire, the other with Marines, and with us on the ridge line, we mortared and shelled the valley. The line company then swept the area. We burned all the villages and engaged in several firefights. Unknown to us the ridge line we were on was heavily booby trapped. We found out in a series of earth-shattering blasts that took the lives of seven Marines. Because the enemy has built fortified positions, we had to delay the operation a week or two.

During these three months that I have been here, my battalion, 3/26, is taking a lot of casualties. In my platoon alone (81s), we have twenty-eight Purple Hearts out of eighty men.

Well, I'll try and write soon.

Daryl

Snipers

The countryside was rife with snipers. They were in trees, in villages and sometimes in spider holes in the ground. They were not all necessarily a crack shot. Once in a while you could hear the wing of a shot go whizzing past.

Easy Capture for "I" Co.

By Cpl. Cal Guthrie

PHU BAI—The capture of a Viet Cong guerrilla ... as the Third Division unit (I company 3/26) neared a bamboo thicket, a man from the company's Second Platoon stumbled in the grass.... Crouched in the tiny cavity (spider hole) was a Viet Cong soldier. (Guthrie, "Easy Capture for 'I' Co.," *Sea Tiger*, 1967)

He was later coaxed out of the hole and interrogated. The ground was rife with these spider holes with VC snipers holed up in them for weeks and months at a time.

Apology
2-18-67

Tell Dad I am trying to handle my Marine Corps career with finesse, and my objective is, of course, college. I am saving money—I really have nowhere to spend it—and with the GI Bill I will have plenty for college. I really don't know how long I'll be here. My tour is up in September sometime, but I might extend. With more rank and a transfer, I think I can manage to get stationed in a much safer place than this.

I have had plenty of time to think about my past and all that was said and done, and I have come to the conclusion (it will sound funny) that you knew what you were talking about. Both you and Dad, with perception that comes with age and experience, analyzed my position and told me the "straight scoop," as we say in the corps. But to a seventeen-year-old with my ambition, who knew everything, this wise advice just didn't register. This, I am afraid, is the closest I can come to an apology for those few years in which you suffered my adolescence. However, I am proud now to be in the Marine Corps and proud to fight for my country and the things you and I believe in, so at least one of my "well thought out" decisions turned out right. I'll write soon.

Love, Daryl

Hot Showers and Hot Meals
2-22-67

I now have enough powdered drinks, cigarettes, toilette gear, and candy and gum to last me a long time, and if I do run out of these items, for the first time, I have a chance to buy them. Remember when I mentioned how this area is being built up? Yesterday we got a permanent PX. Today they set up tents and put in hot showers, and next week they are reopening the beer hall. What else could a man ask for? It makes me wonder because, as I told you before, there was nothing but grass, hills, and VC when the battalion arrived.

The only things I can't really get hold of are cigars and your cookies and fudge (of course) and sardines. Also, I forgot to mention, four days ago they set up a mess hall too, and we now get two hot meals a day. So they really are taking care of me.

I guess all these things come with the start of Chinook II. We finished Chinook I, the first phase in securing this area. Chinook II, which will last to the middle of March or the first of April, will consist of securing the rest of the valley. During this second phase, 1/9, another battalion and fourth regiment headquarters have moved in. After this phase is complete we will move into the mountains.

The irony of it all is when we left the mouth of the river, when we first came "in-country," this operation was only to last fourteen days. But since we were so successful, it seems the plans have changed and it was decided to secure the whole area for keeps. Well, I'll write soon. Meanwhile, everyone please take care.

Daryl

More Slack
2-26-67

I have some good news. In a couple of weeks, after we kick off the second phase of Chinook, our battalion will be pulled out to a secure area (Phu Bai) for a little "slack," meaning rest. The reason for us being pulled back is that we have seen more than our share of combat and hardships in relation to the other existing Marine battalions over here.

I am in province Thua Thien, District Phong Dien, Area Coby Ton Ton. Province=Tinh; District=Quan. This should help you locate me.

I now have a stable routine. It consists of eating twice a day, taking a shower, standing four hours of radio watch, and practicing on the mortar. Mortar training is not required; in fact, only the radio watch is mandatory, but it is something I am doing for the sake of knowledge and experience. I am now efficient at any aspect of the 81 platoon and fire the mortar and help plot for actual missions. But this will soon cease because I think I will again have to go back out as FO.

Daryl

Death and Survival

Despite the interlude the war continued to heat up. The illusion of success was very powerful. The enemy was dogged, but not invincible, or so we thought. The Viet Cong were worthy partners in this game of blood, sweat, earth, and fear. But out of a growing respect for the enemy came an appreciation of our warrior skills. They were good but we were better. I reveled in this ability. I felt confident in myself and in some of the other Marines who had been tested in combat. I waited silently for the next battle by cleaning my weapon, improving my skills, and checking and rechecking my gear. I spent many hours optimizing my load by carefully choosing my tools of death and survival.

Court Martial
2-27-67

I was up most of the night last night because we were on 100 percent alert. We received information from a dozen VC POWs in the prison compound fifty meters from my bunker. They said that 81s would be mortared at 2100 hours. We never were.

Yesterday a corporal and PFC were busted at a court martial for firing the wrong direction with the mortar. These two guys were pretty close friends of mine and it happened when I got off watch (I was A-gunner), and the next round they fired as I walked into the bunker turned out to be in the wrong direction. Lucky no friendlies were hurt or they probably would be behind bars.

I'll write soon.
Daryl.

Jail in the 'Nam

I was very afraid of going to jail. Not that I did anything to warrant this but it was something to consider. It could happen by striking a green officer or even having sharp words. Outside of being killed, captured, or maimed, the only thing worse than what I was already enduring was going to prison in Vietnam. It was purposefully horrifying to keep the discipline.

Fudge Allotment
3-4-67

I received two more packages and both were completely fresh. One was of your marvelous fudge. And the other contained some much-needed socks and my favorite salami. The troops in my squad want to sign this letter in appreciation for the limited amount of fudge I allot to them. They refuse to thank me, but they are more than glad to thank you.

As for you, Mom, it doesn't bother me if you are sentimental and serious. I am able to understand your feelings quite well. Those pictures were nice, but it looks like you sent me the worst of the lot. I don't blame you, but I can't even tell if Kita has a face or if Sam has any expression. But they will do ...

About those pictures I was going to send. I gave the box to my buddy when I was on ship. He said he would mail it, but we were separated from our sea bags where he put it, and then he was transferred to 3/4. Yesterday 3/4 got overrun, sustaining many casualties. I am not too sure that he is alive, so I don't know what will happen to the package.

Daryl

Hurry up and Wait
3-15-67

This is just a short line to maintain correspondence. Right now I am on watch. Also, I am on five-minute standby as FO (forward observer) for operation Sparrow Hawk. This is a reactionary force that will be flown to any hot spot in Vietnam by chopper. I am really not too worried about being constantly ready. For one thing, I have been on several of these. In fact, I was supposed to be completely ready in full gear in support of an ARVN operation. Instead, I was sunbathing, knowing full well that five minutes means one to two hours. Not that I don't believe we will be called on, for I have many times been called while on standby, but the Marine Corps follows one rule: "Hurry up and wait," and this never varies. The reason is the human error in chain of command.

When General says five-hour notice, the PFC hears five to ten seconds, giving everyone a buffer.

I have everything I could want here: EM [enlisted men's] club, movie, hot showers, PX, bookstores, post office, and chow hall; all the comforts of garrison. We should be moving out of Phu Bai, in another month and a half. They say Da Nang or possibly Chu Lai is next, but I don't know for sure. It really is late, 2:30 a.m., so goodbye for now. I hope you are all well.

Daryl

In the Rear with the Gear
3-14-67

I am now in Phu Bai; though I am still collecting combat pay, I am technically in garrison rather than war. Believe it or not I have turned in all my ammo and grenades and bandoleers and I am not even required to wear body armor (e.g., flak jacket or helmet). We saw more than our share of action and now they have pulled us back to this secured area where all we do is eat, sleep, and stand inspections. Actually, I have gone too far. Our guns are set up and we still fire missions.... I am here in fire direction control in front of an arsenal of communications gear supervising the whole mess by the marvels of electronics.

Chinook was unique in the operational history of the armed services participating in this fiasco of a war. Our battalion was face-to-face with the enemy and weather all alone in an area that had never been occupied by friendly troops for any extended period. The area was a thoroughly VC-infested district and was consequently designated a free killing zone. However ominous this sounds, it was a thousand-fold worse for the troops who conquered the area. As reward the high command has disarmed us and put us in sanitary, weatherproof buildings, ordered us into starched utilities, and prepared us for a forthcoming parade—mind you, a parade with spit-shined boots and all the trimmings.

Personally, I couldn't care less. I have no gear to speak of, combat loss, so I cannot keep spit and polish on something I do not have. Also, I am still functional in the war effort as far as killing the enemy, although it is quite indirect, sitting on a phone quite a distance from action. But really, I wish I was back in Chinook or in the field where I am in front of the enemy and know what the scoop is from being there, not through rumor or phone lines. I imagine as the petty things become more and more important I and everyone else will be begging to go back to the field.

So here I am in the rear with the gear. The whole battalion pulled out of a unique position of personally fighting the enemy on their own ground, to a position that 99 percent of all the other troops occupy, and that is the rear. It seems it takes all of Phu Bai and all of Dong Ha to support one lousy battalion in the field.

Do you realize that these 99 percent have never even seen the enemy or fired a round or thrown a grenade in combat? Do you realize that they have been safe and are under the impression of fighting a war? Well, now I am safe. But I don't like it.

Daryl

Even the Rear Is in the Front

"Only a minority has actually clashed with large Vietnamese units or Vietcong irregulars, run into mines or booby traps, or been ambushed" (Karnow, 1991).

On the other hand everyone in the rear was subjected to enemy mortar fire. No one was ever safe.

News Interview

Well, we received more replacements. These guys are worse than the last ones. But really, they're all the same. As a matter of fact, this set came in the Marine Corps in October '66. This means I was overseas before these people were even in the corps.

This morning I was interviewed and made a tape recording with a news service reporter for a news broadcast. If by chance they play it on one of our hometown stations, they will contact you and tell you the time so you can listen.

Daryl

Dangerous Haircut

Before I was interviewed I wanted to clean up. Getting a haircut and a shave was a real experience. The Vietnamese barbers would cut your hair with long pointed scissors and shave your face and throat with a sharp open-edged razor. The shave was followed by a hot towel on your face so you could not see. This was especially harrowing, as everyone suspected they were VCs at night. It was a funny badge of courage to get your haircut. At the end of the haircut they would hold your head and move it side to side and then abruptly crack it with a forceful jerk.

Fear of Burning

3/14/1967

Dear Colette,

The operation I was on, Chinook I and II, is now being conducted by First Bn Ninth Marines, and we are now in Phu Bai more or less regrouping and getting resupplied, plus getting in a little rest. However, we still are on standby for several operations and are responsible for the security of the base and airstrip.

I am presently on watch at 81 mortar fire direction control. I just received a call from the Fire Support Control Center to fire a mission of illumination because of enemy activity on the perimeter. I took the grids and checked my logs and charts, located the gun to shoot and then radioed the fire mission. This might sound exciting, but this is an hourly occurrence on night watch.

As you have probably gathered, I am no longer at the working end (forward observer) but am presently in fire direction control, the other end, so to speak. In other words, I used to request and observe where now I receive and decide. The latter is much safer.

In your letter you wondered if I am getting white hairs right now compared to when I was in very little danger. However, when you received my previous letter I was at Chinook, and although I personally do not sport white hairs, a few of my comrades do.

We are using napalm and white phosphorous whenever possible. The Viet Cong are deadly afraid of burning. Napalm … can … be delivered by plane. I have personally [called in] several air strikes on Viet Cong with a special request for napalm.

In this instance, I was approximately three hundred-fifty meters away on a hill observation post where we could observe Viet Cong at a distance and call in suitable fire, whether air, artillery, or my 81 mortars depending on distance and availability.

As for public opinion and student demonstrations about the war, it personally doesn't bother me, but I have seen an adverse effect on my fellow Marines. The thing that worries them the most is those few instances where a Marine or soldier from Vietnam steps off of a plane, after being away for so long, and gets shot by a protester or falls and breaks his neck.

You asked me my opinion of the war. My feelings are probably different than others here, but I couldn't say, because this subject is taboo by unwritten law. But when I walk through a poor farm village, rifle locked and loaded, at the ready—or ride through a city in a convoy with rifle locked and loaded, at the ready, or out on an OP (observation post) with rifle locked and loaded, I feel that I am really not part of the people-to-people program.

And when I get shot at, I don't really care if it is a woman or child, VC or not. I shoot back. Horrible yes, but necessary for survival.

You ask me how I feel, and I say when I look at these small people and I get the weird impression that possibly the French might have had the same feelings toward the Nazis when they invaded their homeland, I don't feel good. And when I look at the land I feel it is unfair to be fighting a war with communism on other than our ground, China's, or Russia's but not this unsuspecting country's ground. And when I think of US history and all that led up to this, I think of our civil war, and I wonder about our foreign involvement.

But beyond all of my feelings, I am here on my own accord. I do not use the excuse that one is forced here by law. We alone control our destiny. There are a million ways to avoid the service and a trillion ways to avoid Vietnam. I passed up many ways of getting out because I didn't want to. The reason for my wanting to be here is hardly patriotic but rather in pursuit of personal ideals and goals. I could explain further and perhaps I might in another letter, but not for now at any rate.

I'll write soon.

Daryl

Sleeping on a Fresh Grave
3-20-67

I find my more comfortable living quarters a lot more suitable than my previous sand bag bunker, which was, in fact, a castle compared to the hand-dug foxhole covered simply by a poncho, which I occupied for three months before. But, if you will recall, I said that I was on garrison mostly and was on short notice standby. It seems I really wasn't too far removed from the field or face-to-face combat, as I mistakenly imagined. I have just come in from the field. It was an all-night ambush where we set in silently after dark on a known Viet Cong crossing. Well aware a person cannot stay awake and alert a whole night, we were put on 50 percent watch. I went to a slightly raised soft mound to catch some needed sleep. When I awoke and the moon was brighter I realized I'd been sleeping on a freshly dug and filled grave. I was surprised, but I could not see troubling my comfortable position by moving.

Nothing occurred that night, but the night before in about the same position the company on ambush got hit, sustaining two dead and several wounded but killing only two of the enemy, with unknown wounded. The radio operator whose place I took on this night's ambush got his antenna shot off, and he asked me if I could take his place, which I did. The night after this (last night) he again went out and they were again hit. This is only an example of how fortunate I have been in many similar experiences (knock on wood).

The weather is finally acting like it is supposed to and it is, at last, hot. I am healthy and await the time that I can come home. At this time I am not sure of my plans as far as Vietnam tour goes, but as soon as I acquire all the needed information I will be able to decide.

With much love and care,
Daryl

Ambush

Being on ambush was a challenge. It was nerve-racking waiting for the enemy. One simultaneously hoped for the enemy to walk into the trap to break the tension and for the enemy to (please, God) miss our spot. I peered out into the night, looking down the path. I imagined the trees moving. I fantasized VC walking down the path. I held on to the cord from the Claymore mines I had set up on the path. I waited.

Ambush Well Set by Company from Twenty-Sixth Marines Near Hue

By Sgt. Roger Ynostroza

PHU BAI—"I heard a cough and the first VC came around a bush. I raised my rifle, let him pass by, and then counted three more," said Marine Private Henry Thinelk. "I nudged the man next to me (and) we counted to four and then opened up ..." Thinelk said. (Ynostroza, "Ambush Well Set by Company from Twenty-Sixth Marines Near Hue," *Sea Tiger*, 1967)

Anatomy of An Ambush

They and the rest of the squad hit the surprised VC with everything they had: machine gun and rifle fire, as well as M-79s and hand grenades. This was a classic ambush. They were lucky in two ways: first it only took fifteen minutes to spring the ambush; and second, it went off without a hitch. Typically one either stared into the darkness so intently that moving shapes appeared, or one felt the overwhelming drug of fatigue and sleepiness. The ambush plan was to hit and run because the size of the enemy force was unknown. So they pulled back and met up with some elements of the platoon. Along with some artillery rounds for good measure, 60mm mortars were laid down beyond the ambush. This was intended to block the escape of the enemy. The area was policed and three guerrillas were found. ... (Ynostroza, 1967)

Locked and Loaded
3-21-67

The other day here in Phu Bai we had a parade that commemorated changing of command in the third division to which we are now attached. Major General Hochmuth, the commanding general from Marine Corps Recruit Depot, San Diego, took over here while the former Third Marine Division commander resumes command of the Fifth Division that is near completing its reactivation. I do not know when we will again be assumed under Fifth Division command.

Also, the other day we had chapel services for those 3/26 dead, twenty-three plus one who had died in an ambush the day before. The ambush started on the second night in Cobi Ton Ton (Chinook). We were hit by a human wave banzai attack as was reported in the paper. One of the sergeants in 81s who at one time was a member of my FO team is now on the Repose (hospital ship) because he cracked up. He was the forward observer. All he could say on the radio was, "Give me light, they just keep coming." They pulled him out and kept him in the rear where he then received notice of his father's death and went on emergency leave. When he came back, he wasn't quite the same. I guess he thought the VC were still coming because when another sergeant went into his hooch, he locked and loaded and almost shot him. So they sent him away.

I hear a rumor that we will leave Phu Bai in the middle of March and go to Da Nang for a while. But I have reason to believe that we will go to the Mekong Delta. There are only two battalions trained to fight under the conditions in the area, 1/9 and 3/26. 1/9 has already been there, but we haven't.

Love, Daryl

Eternal Rest

Memorial service pamphlet dated March 17, 1967:

> Men of the Third Battalion, Twenty-Sixth Marines who have died in action:

Cpl. R. Ratcliff, I Co; Sgt. S. F. Jalloway, I Co; LCpl. P. O. Evans, L Co; PFC T. W. Shalhoob, K Co; PFC M. Vasquez, K Co; Cpl. G. T. Schneider, L Co; HN R. W. Green, H&S Co; LCpl. J. A. Abrams, I Co; PFC T. A. Greg, I Co; PFC R. B. Painter, K Co; LCpl. F Hummingbird, L Co; LCpl. K. W. Kraus, L Co; HN C F. Fincher, H&S Co; HN W. A. Beyer, I Co; LCpl. D. J. Frischmann, M. Co; Sgt. L. Robinson Jr., M Co; PFC C. M. Swain, H&S Co; Sgt. M. E. Burns, K Co; Capt. R. E. Hines, I Co; Sgt. D. F. Kaufman, M Co; PFC R. L. Thornell, M Co; PFC G. R. Worrell, I Co; LCpl. F. J. Berry Jr., M Co.

Eternal rest grant unto them, O Lord. May they rest in peace!

The Marine Prayer:

Almighty Father, whose command is over all and whose love never fails, make me aware of thy presence and obedient to thy will.

Keep me true to my best self, guarding me against dishonesty in purpose and deed and helping me to live so that I can face my fellow Marines, my loved ones, and thee without shame or fear.

Protect my family.

Give me the will to do the work of a Marine and to accept my share of responsibilities with vigor and enthusiasm.

Grant me the courage to be proficient in my daily performance.

Keep me loyal and faithful to my superiors and to the duties my country and the Marine Corps have entrusted in me.

Make me considerate of those committed to my leadership.

Help me wear my uniform with dignity and let it remind me daily of the traditions which I must uphold.

If I am inclined to doubt, steady my faith; if I am tempted, make me strong to resist; if I should miss the mark, give me the courage to try again.

Guide me with the light of truth and grant me the wisdom by which I may understand the answer to my prayer. Amen.

Written on many flak jackets and helmets:

Yeah though I walk through the valley of death, I shall fear no evil, because I am the meanest mother fucker in the valley.

Words from the Marine Corps hymn:

If the army and the navy ever looked on heaven's scenes, they will find the streets guarded by United States Marines.

We have a motto that sums it all up: all gave some; some gave all.
—Howard Osterkamp of Dent,
Korean War veteran
Commander of Chapter 3620
The Military Order of the Purple Heart

It Seems like It's Over

I felt a sense of completion. I had been in combat a number of times and felt I had all the experience I needed. I could go home now and feel proud of what I'd survived. As the memorial proved, I had been lucky. Unfortunately my tour was not up until September and it was only March. Little did I know a terrible time still awaited me in the field. A succession of battles and combat would sap my spirit and destroy my youthful smugness.

The Street without Joy

3-22-67

Enclosure—Leatherneck Fire Team Phrase Book (e.g., Handling prisoners: Drop your weapon = day shoomswong).

Below is a clipping from the *Sea Tiger* (Amphibious Task Force unit paper), USMC. I was on that "street without joy" discussed in the article, and believe me, it is more than they say. They don't mention 3/26 in Chinook II, but we started Chinook II and then turned it over to 1/9 and 2/9.

Oddly enough I would soon be transferred to the 2/9 outfit.

"Street without Joy" Lives up to Its Name

By SSgt. Norman W. MacKenzie

PHU BAI—The "Street without Joy" lived up to its title when Third Division Marines encountered a virtual fortress. Fourteen years ago Dr. Bernard Fall named the street when thirty thousand French troops fought the Viet Minh there. Since Fall's book and the departure of French troops, the area has been primarily controlled [and heavily fortified] by an enemy battalion." (MacKenzie, "Street without Joy Lives Up to Its Name," *Sea Tiger*, 1967)

Dr. Fall was killed that day and on that street he'd so aptly named. He was killed by a "bouncing betty" mine that was tripped near him. It was a hellish way to die first invented by the Germans.

The author went on to describe an enemy-fortified Viet Cong village, typical of what we often ran into on enemy sweeps. The village was replete with bunkers, arms, food caches, and ammunition and it was surrounded by mines, booby traps, punji pits, and fighting holes.

We were in support of this operation, and the death of Dr. Fall seemed like an eerie warning from the French past. We could not befall the same fate as we were US Marines—or so our youth led us to believe.

Like most of the time during sweeps, the days would wear on, punctuated by a solitary blast of a tripped mine or booby trap, and the anguished muffled screams of the bravely wounded. The obligatory medevac would follow and we would avert our eyes and minds from the truth and soldier on.

Humping
4-18-67

I just got back from ten days in the field, which is the reason you haven't received any mail. When I got in, I got your two packages, one with the canned goods and the other with nuts. This will, indeed, come in handy, for tomorrow I go to Hill 180, a gun position where I will have only C-rations again. But really, it won't be so bad because everything else is beautiful.

About those ten days in the field, I must say they were the worst I have had in Vietnam. Altogether we suffered four dead, twenty

A Hellish Place of Angels

wounded. We got six VC and an unknown number wounded. What it amounted to was one company plus one section of 81s. We mounted out with two 81 rounds (twenty-two pounds), a radio or piece of the gun (twenty-three to forty-five pounds), a case of C-rations (twenty-five pounds), pack, rifle, helmet, flak jacket, and ammunition (about twenty-five pounds). So each man was carrying about one hundred pounds of gear, if not more, and we humped, or rather struggled, sixty thousand meters all told, always moving at night or dusk. We humped to the base of the mountains to set up an elaborate ambush.

Our company moved into an area where thirteen men from recon were operating, and they became attached. The VC controlled the mountains and the piedmont. That night the VC hit the recon unit, killing one, wounding the other twelve as well as killing their dog, a German shepherd Marine Corps hound. The bullets from the fight were hitting our area. It was pretty messy. Later that night we were hit again and the VC overran the perimeter of our ambush. We threw up all the illumination we had and were sitting on needles till a 'copter came in and resupplied us in a combination medevac and emergency supply.

After that night we were hit five times in ten days. From the beginning of this ten-day field trip I swam in the South China Sea and ended up in the mountains. ... We are operating a little north of Da Nang. The only trouble I had personally was leeches. I think I lost a half pint of blood to the dozen or so leeches I acquired. Bullets and field no longer bother me, but after the third day I had to abandon my radio at the Cac 7 Marine Corps ARVN outpost because I loaned workable parts to air control and the company radio operator. I then became a grunt (infantry man) and ammo humper. I carried four rounds, forty-four pounds, and the tube or base plate, twenty-six to twenty-eight pounds. The walking was hard all over. Plus I stood perimeter watch every night and ambush [in the] day.

It's all over now, so no sweat. I'll write when I get to hill 180, my next stop.

Daryl

That Fucking PRC

Humping a PRC 25 radio, or prick 25, as it was affectionately called, was difficult for two reasons. It was very heavy—about twenty-six pounds plus five pounds for an extra battery, and it made you a target. Second only to officers, radio operators had a shorter life span in battle than those in any other occupation. The Viet Cong were experienced, hardened fighters. They knew the value of cutting off communications and support. And I knew they knew. It was very hard to camouflage a radio. It was very big, much bigger than it needed to be. The ten-foot whip antenna was impossible to hide. I almost never used it unless ordered to do so. There was a metal tape antenna I kept folded over my shoulder and tucked into my webbing. Still, any VC could see I was a radio operator. One thing it did do was cover my back. On more than one occasion the radio stopped small pieces of shrapnel.

If the radio was all I carried that would have been enough. But it wasn't. In no particular order I almost always wore or carried:

- Jungle boots
- Jungle pants with no underwear
- Webbed cartridge belt with combat suspenders
- Three canteens of water
- K-bar knife and scabbard
- Flak jacket
- Helmet, liner, cover, and band
- Dog tags
- Zippo lighter
- E-tool

A Hellish Place of Angels

- Poncho
- Cigarettes
- Radio plus webbed harness
- Extra battery
- Socks
- Jungle jacket
- Green T-shirt
- A green towel
- Bayonet and scabbard
- M 14 or M 16 rifle
- Bandoleer of ammo
- Haversack
- 1/4 stick of plastic explosive
- Four to six cans of C-rations (sometimes a case)
- Water treatment pills
- Toothbrush
- Toilet paper
- Paper and pen
- Flashlight
- Blousing bands for pants
- 45-caliber pistol and holster
- Battle dressings
- Insect repellent
- One to two smoke grenades
- Two to three hand grenades
- One willy peter (white phosphorous) grenade
- Four loaded magazines of ammo for my rifle
- Four loaded magazines for my pistol
- Map
- Gas mask (rarely)
- One or two mortar rounds (rarely)
- A claymore mine (rarely)

- Salt tabs when ordered to do so
- Letters from home
- Other miscellaneous and personal affects

In today's digital and wireless world only a few can understand how big and heavy the "prick" radio was.

At the end of each day's march, if we went through rice paddies or a river, I would check my legs by rolling up my jungle pants. My pant legs were bloused against a band to prevent insects from crawling up. This was no protection against leeches. Several times when I checked, giant leeches gorged with my blood would fall to the ground and wiggle. They were too full to hang on. I'd never felt them. The idea of them made me sick.

Once we were on a long march in the heat and I was out of water. I was desperate. The only water was a muddy hole everyone ahead of me had stomped through. I filled my canteen, using my fingers to keep out the muck and then treated the water with iodine tablets. I took a drink and a leech flopped around in my mouth. I spat it out. It was already big, so it may have gorged on someone else's blood.

The terrain we trekked through was beautiful and rural. We would walk in a long column through peaceful lush rice paddies and spot the occasional water buffalo. The serenity would be pierced by a burst of fire or a booby trap exploding, triggered by anyone in the column or sometimes triggered on command by a watching VC.

Booby traps often caused terrible wounds and chipped at the morale of the troops. One of the most feared booby traps was a "bouncing betty," an explosive projectile that would be launched from the ground three to six feet in the air. The damage it caused was horrendous. It essentially was a mortar shell rigged from a buried tube and set to go off immediately. Unlike a mortar, you could not get down and escape the blast zone. The blast itself came down. One officer was considerate enough to take a bouncing betty under his flak jacket. No one else was injured because his jacket and his chest shielded others from the blast, but were, in turn, shredded in the process. It was an ugly way to die.

I constantly looked for a trip wire, disturbed ground, or disturbed leaves. Others walked in a daze waiting to stop for a rest. They were tired and soon would be injured or dead. Vietnam was unforgiving.

Everywhere I went the fucking PRC was there hanging on to my every step and every word.

Light a New Day
Dear Colette,

I come from the worst and I am now at the best. From a mission that seemed only to deal with the fact of my existence to a position and situation of sanctity. Presently I am on hill 180 with my gun crew. Hill 180 is an observation post and mortar position for the defense of Phu Bai. The hill rates one 81 mortar, one 106 recoilless, and a squad of grunts.

It affords a view of the South China Sea, all of Phu Bai and with a turn of the head, the Laotian border. The solitude and beautiful view of this hill bring a touch of unreality and detachment that is essential for relaxation and thought. Here I am unwinding from an escapade that was far worse than any I have seen since I have been in Vietnam.

We have one squad (one gun and seven people) and me. I am second senior in command and help the squad leader (corporal) compute fire missions plus maintain communications. We also have a squad of grunts as security, plus an army installation for top secret radio relay. The hill is about fifty meters by one hundred fifty meters and we live in close quarters but are surrounded by barbed wire and signs.

Believe it or not, the responsibility feels good and the lack of unnecessary authority is great. The only setback is the food, C-rations, but after all this time we have become adept at making it tasty or at least edible.

The funny thing up here is the toilet. Oddly enough it is mounted in the open on the highest knoll so when you sit on it you can see a hundred miles in all directions. Presumably the enemy can see you too.

For entertainment yesterday, I went down the hill to the ARVN compound and made arrangements for myself and the seven others in our team to come on base and go to their E club. With a Vietnamese translation card, my little knowledge of French and their little knowledge of English, I was able to conduct business in a tri-language system with a few helpers using universal sign language. The Army of the Republic of Vietnam (ARVN) gents are really quite decent and they even offered to bring beer and ice every day to our hill, plus provide an occasional trip to Hue for fun.

I must sign off; the sun is coming up once again to light a new day. Things must be done, which I must do and I'll write again.

Daryl

PS We have two dogs up here, Alice and Ralph.

Future Plans
Dear Family,
    When the two-year college equivalency test comes out, I will take it for GP (general principle). When I get back I am requesting Lejeune Marine Corps Base, North Carolina, which has part of North Carolina University right on base and has a fabulous program for Marines who wish to go who are on the base. Also, it would give me a chance to see New York and Washington DC while on

liberty. It seems I could soak up some credits and also travel a little while still in the Marine Corps. I have a still insatiable passion to see Europe but I will postpone it till I am a civilian, possibly as a foreign exchange student.

I'll write soon.

Front Teeth
4-27-67

Nothing new is happening really. This is just a short letter to let you know I am still in good health. While I have a chance I am going to get some work done on my teeth. I don't think I ever told you, but I chipped my front tooth again, just the porcelain on the bridge, during a firefight. I guess it's just a bad habit. It really isn't too important over here because looks aren't much good for anything. Also, I want to go to Da Nang and get my eyes examined and get some new glasses. Today I took a final exam for a Marine Corps correspondence course. It was no sweat. It will help me get my next rank. I hope everything is fine and that you are celebrating a pleasant Passover.

Love Daryl

Held Together with Tape and Chewing Gum
My front teeth were knocked out several times when I was younger to the point that I had a bridge. This bridge was shattered from a bullet fragment early in my tour. It was an old-fashioned bridge and had a post that held the porcelain cap. The post was tearing and rubbing raw the tender flesh on the inside of my upper lip. To prevent this, I wore an old piece of chewing gum between my teeth and my lip. My glasses were also broken and taped together.

I Must Be Lucky
5-1-67

Again I am in the field, this time for thirty days, on Operation Golden Fleece, to protect the villagers and rice during harvest time from VC. Remember the clipping you sent me about Marines set up in small groups right inside the village protecting the villagers? Well, we have moved into one south of Phu Bai and are doing what the clipping implied. We sleep in an old French fort. I managed to procure a cot from the area, and I sleep in comfort while everyone else looks on in envy. We are right by a river so we can go swimming. Also, with the village all around us, we can manage to be invited for dinner. Even fried rice and rat meat is better than C-rations, and I am an expert with chop sticks.

You probably heard that Phu Bai was hit by mortars and small arms. This happened the night before we left. I tell you, I must be lucky. The mortars kept coming closer and then skipped my position to go on again afterward. Our CO got hit in the head and so did our first sergeant, plus sixty-five other casualties. Nobody really got hurt seriously, though we lost the mess hall and six vehicles. The mess hall can be repaired.

Daryl

Grenade Toss Plus

I was extremely lucky. I had several memorable close calls. Once we were in a grenade fight. We were tossing grenades at the enemy and they were tossing their grenades (and ours that were thrown too quickly) at us. An enemy grenade landed right next to me and didn't go off. I looked right at it before it rolled away.

B-52 bombers were carpet bombing the supply trails at some distance from our position. You could hear them and see them in the distance. The explosions from the two-thousand-pound bombs they dropped were enormous and vibrated through the earth like an earthquake. A steel chunk the size of a fist came soaring out of nowhere to smack into the mud next to me.

I used to pick pieces of shrapnel out of my flak jacket from time to time. For a long time little pieces of shrapnel would work their way out of my arms and legs.

The Best Teacher Is Experience
5-2-67

As I wrote in my last letter, we are now on a thirty-day problem (Operation Golden Fleece) and are working in conjunction with the ARVN, PFs, and villagers. We are set in an old French fort. Working with the Vietnamese and the Vietnam army is old hat to me and a few of my friends, but now most everyone in our platoon is brand new, "green" replacements.

So I live in comfort, swim every day, eat and drink beer while almost everyone else who doesn't know what is happening is miserable. I try to help them but the best teacher is experience. Also, I am now the computer for the section. In other words, we have a new section leader and he doesn't know anything about mortars, so I have to plot the missions on the plotting board and work up the data for the guns. Last night I fired several combat missions and was complimented on accuracy and speed by the captain.

If I do come home after my tour, which is most likely, I will get a twenty-day leave as soon as I get stateside.

I'll write soon. Daryl

Explosive Shit

I got so cocky on the guns that on one occasion I refused to fire a mission ordered by the sergeant because I knew it was wrong. I am sure I saved some lives, but I had also disobeyed an order and had argued with a superior. For punishment, I was sent to burn "honey pots" for a day. Honey pots was our affectionate term for outhouses that had removable drums to collect the waste. My job was to remove the full barrels, mix them with diesel fuel, burn the waste to ashes, and then bury the ashes. I couldn't understand the rationale except that the Vietnamese didn't want any more of our shit than they absolutely had to have.

I went to check out some jerry cans filled with diesel fuel. I took them to the pots and stirred the fuel into the shit as thoroughly as possible. I remember looking at the waste and marveling how many different varieties there were, given we were all eating the same thing. *Well, that's what I get for having a Jewish mother who is a nurse*, I remember thinking.

After the mix was well stirred, I took some rolled newspaper and lit it like a torch. I bent over close to light it, as diesel can be tricky to light. It blew up with an enormous whoosh. I had gotten gas instead of diesel! The explosion had knocked me on my butt, burnt off my eyebrows and some of my hair, and given me first- and second-degree burns on my face and arms—not to mention the fact that there was shit everywhere.

As there was some concern about infection from the crap all over me, I was sent to medical to wash and to bandage my burns. After repairs, I was sent back to my unit as a pathetic Marine, wrapped in gauze, who couldn't even burn shit correctly.

By this time my unit had shipped out to the bush so I was taken by helicopter to their location, bandages and all. There were strict orders about qualifying for sick bay. I can remember fighting with the gauze on and redressing my burns in the field.

Since the battalion came over intact everyone's tour would expire on the same date, thus effectively eliminating the battalion or creating a battalion of almost all green troops. So it was decided to begin transfers of men to other units and slowly replace the battalion to provide a better transition.

From the Ocean to the Border

Transfers are starting to come through. Today I am going into "town" (Phu Bai) to take a test for a Marine Corps correspondence course. As far as the future, our battalion is leaving here in about two-and-a-half weeks, either to Da Nang or a new operation. Already I have been on five combat operations, Chinook, Chinook II, Prairie, Big Horn, and Golden Fleece. I have been from the DMZ to Da Nang, from the ocean to the border.

    Daryl

Bad Water

There were a lot of things I did not write home about. This was especially true about my health because my mother was a nurse and a Jewish mother at that. She worried incessantly about all of the possible diseases her children could get. And naturally, so did her children.

    There are few experiences worse than being sick in Vietnam in the field. One time our company got bad water and we were all sick. A huge hole was dug to hold our waste. The worst of us could not leave the sick tents that were set up. They just exploded from both ends with every drink of water. They certainly could take no food and were too weak to move. In the beginning, we were sent charcoal pills, peanut butter, and clean water. Apparently this was more expedient than medevacing the entire company. They were out of anti-diarrhea medication and eventually could not supply us any medication at all. We ended up making our own charcoal in small day fires.

    I had fever, chills, and the trots. I felt very vulnerable. No matter what, I tried to take care of my feet. A Marine's feet are only second in importance to his rifle. Despite my best efforts large pieces of white dead flesh could be pulled off from time to time.

One evening there was word that we could expect a massive attack. Volunteers were sought to go to reinforce the perimeter. No one volunteered for a few incredible seconds, and then I raised my hand. Soon others volunteered and we were sent to the line. All night I stayed awake waiting for the cans on the concertina wire to rattle. I spent all night seeing shadows and calling for illumination rounds. All night and nothing happened.

In the morning I was promoted to corporal and transferred out of my unit to one that was leaving Vietnam. It was a solution to a sticky problem. I had disobeyed orders but had shown some leadership. The solution: promote and transfer.

2nd Battalion 9th Marines Patch

Good News
5-5-67

At last I have some news that you'll be very happy to hear. For one thing, my transfer finally came through and by the twelfth of May I'll be in 2/9 (Second Battalion, Ninth Marines). Everyone in Vietnam wants a transfer to 2/9 and I got it. The reason: they are going to Okinawa for SLF (remember, this is what I was on when I first came over, Special Landing Force). So by May 15 or so I will be out of Vietnam for at least three months, probably till the end of my tour. I'll still be collecting combat pay because for several days out of each month we float offshore of Vietnam and then go back to Okinawa or the Philippines. How does that sound?

Also, I finally picked up corporal, you know, noncommissioned officer. [Hand drawing of stripes were in the letter.] When I get my warrant, I'll tell you when you can change from L/Cpl to Cpl in your address on my letters. This rank means more money and less work, and that appeals to me. Making this rank almost guarantees my becoming a sergeant before I get out of the corps.

I hope you'll enjoy this news as much as I do.

Daryl

Did I Actually Think I Could Ever Go Home?

The good news about 2/9, like so much else in Vietnam, turned out to be bum scoop. President Johnson was making some bold decisions about the war. 2/9 was destined for some of the worst fighting yet in Vietnam. We were being sent to the heart of the battle zone: the DMZ. But there was no "we." I would be new to the 2/9 battalion. Experienced, combat tested but still an unknown. Robert S. McNamara, Secretary of Defense, thought we were all identical and replaceable cogs in a giant machine. Not so.

I doubted very much I would ever make it home again.

Part IV

Into the Zone

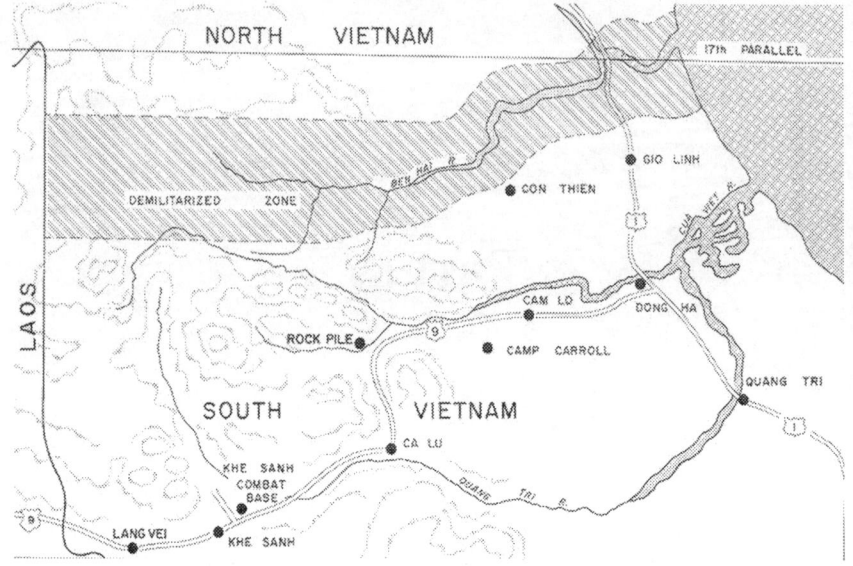

The DMZ

DMZ

The DMZ began as a neutral no-man's-land to provide a negotiated buffer between the two Vietnams. However, in 1967 the DMZ evolved into a death zone where the Third Marine Division faced off with multiple divisions of the North Vietnamese Army (NVA) in a series of savage and brutal contests with thousands of casualties on both sides. I was there during this mayhem.

Three miles deep on either side of the border between the China Sea and the Laotian frontier is the strip of land known as the Demilitarized Zone (DMZ). Established at the Geneva Conference in 1954.... For almost a year now ... the North Vietnamese regulars [have been] sifting through it or using it as a base from which to attack US Marines to the south. ("DMZ," *Newsweek*, 1967)

A Hellish Place of Angels

"DMZ" Something of a Misnomer

SAIGON (AP)—Only in name is it a Demilitarized Zone. At least three Communist divisions operate within the zone. Much of the recent fighting has centered there or in that vicinity.... In recent months the DMZ has become the hottest war zone in Vietnam. (Faas, "'DMZ' Something of a Misnomer," *Pacific Stars and Stripes,* 1967)

The DMZ divided North Vietnam from South Vietnam and represented a line in the sand for the US forces and another way into South Vietnam for the North Vietnamese.

The Third Marine Division, with South Vietnamese troops (including my units 3/26 and 2/9), fought south of the DMZ for many months before breaching the perceived sanctity of the zone. We went into the DMZ to help protect our northernmost bases and to rout out the tenacious enemy who had infiltrated across the border into South Vietnam.

The DMZ slices through the country in consort with the Ben Hai River. Highway 1, which travels north to south and formerly connected Saigon with Hanoi, crossed the Ben Hai river via the "Freedom Bridge." On one occasion we were close enough to the bridge to see, with binoculars, the policemen from both countries guarding the bridge. The railroad that ran along route 1 was no longer in operation as the rails were targeted for scrap and war production.

The Third Marine Division set up four strong points in the lowlands of the eastern part of the DMZ called Leatherneck Square where there was concentrated heavy artillery, troops, armor, and supplies. The square was made up of Con Thien and Gio Linh, six miles apart as the northern line and Dong Ha and Cam Lo together as the southern line nine miles to the south. Some of the heaviest fighting of the war was in this fifty–four-square-mile area in the shadow of the DMZ.

The Third Mar Div set up its forward headquarters in Dong Ha, which was heavily fortified. The post contained an air strip for C130 planes and advanced radar to control bombing missions. Dong Ha was our rear area which was farther forward then almost any other unit's forward position. Despite the heavy fortifications Dong Ha was attacked with mortars on more than one occasion. In one attack my personal records and belongings were destroyed.

Con Thien and Gio Linh were attacked every day with enemy rockets, artillery, and mortars. Con Thien bore the brunt of the enemy's wrath arguably more than any other US military post.

Con Thien was on the Western edge of a twelve mile bulldozed line as part of the now militarized zone. Residents in the area were resettled elsewhere and the area was deemed a free fire zone. Vegetation was killed with Agent Orange. This was called the McNamara wall in honor of the Secretary of Defense Robert McNamara. While it represented a massive effort, the enemy was not playing by the same rule book. The NVA just went around the obstacles. Clearly the top brass was still fighting the last war.

In 1967 Con Thien was brutally attacked on multiple occasions above and beyond the daily shelling. On May 8, the day after the anniversary of Dien Bien Phu, Con Thien was attacked with NVA ground forces soon after the shelling stopped. These attacks escalated throughout the year culminating in a savage clash in September 1967.

Khe Sanh

Con Thien awaited the arrival of my being. I was transferred to 2/9 in early May of 1967 when an element of 2/9 guarded the perimeter of Khe Sanh during the hill fights. (Murphy, 2003)

The DMZ originated in the lowlands, cut through the underbrush to the jungle of the piedmont, and ended in the mountains. Khe Sanh combat base anchored the western portion of the DMZ defensive positions. In the vicinity of Khe Sanh the foot hills 861, 881S and

A Hellish Place of Angels

881N became the next nexus for bitter fighting early in 1967 designed to disrupt the new NVA 325th Division positions. The hill fights, as they are known, were the first battles of Khe Sanh. The NVA's goal was to counter the DMZ build up and get control of Route 9. The Third Marine Division took heavy casualties but secured the hill tops. The year we Marines first fought the well equipped and well trained North Vietnamese army in earnest was 1967. The DMZ grew to mythic proportions as the casualties mounted. The DMZ did not represent a defensive wall to us Marines but rather a killing ground of horror, blood, and honor.

Khe Sanh: The Early Battles, aka the Hill Fights

Hills 881 and 861 were strategic hills in the area of Khe Sanh. Their number designations stood for their elevations in meters. A fierce battle was fought by elements of the Third Marine Division to secure these hills. The battle appeared in *LIFE* magazine ("Khe Sanh: The Hill Battles," 1967). Khe Sanh was a Marine Corps base located in the northwestern sector of South Vietnam, approximately six miles from the Laotian border and about fourteen miles south of the DMZ. Khe Sanh was surrounded by tall, tree-canopied hills, some more than three thousand feet in elevation. Khe Sanh overlooked Route 9, the main eastward entryway from Laos into South Vietnam's northern coastal region. Of course, early the next year (1968) Khe Sanh was encircled by the North Vietnamese divisions, marking one of the defining moments of the war. We were present and accounted for in the early battles for those hills. Typically though I hardly ever knew exactly where I was fighting until after it was over. One thing for sure, there is little worse than struggling up a jungle-covered mountain in the sun or the rain fully loaded with gear, in pursuit of the enemy.

What follows is a rough description of the destructive chaos of 1967 that informed my experience in the second half of my tour of duty.

The Jungle

The last letter I wrote about twelve days ago I told you some interesting things, but everything has changed. I have just gotten back from the jungle in the mountains on the Laotian border, ten days of walking in the steaming heat with vines and leeches. I thought I would never get out. The jungle is like a living creature, and it just won't let you go. The two days before that I was in the process of being transferred from 3/26 to 2/9. This is the first time I could write.

I told you I made corporal, which I did, but I am not going to Okinawa. Things have blown up here in Vietnam. Today 1/9 got hit hard and it looks like things will be rough. We had to cancel Okinawa because we are moving into Khe Sanh (DMZ) where things are too "hot." The North Vietnamese regulars and maybe some Chinese advisors are moving in and we are not fighting guerillas anymore. My new address is:

Corporal Eigen
2nd Bn 9th Marines H & S Co
FMF FPO San Francisco, CA 96602

The only thing different is the rank and the battalion: 2/9 instead of 3/26.

Although my mail will still get here, I already received a package (Kosher cookies) and a letter, but this new address will speed it up beau coup fast. I received your tape and listened to it and felt very good. I wish I could send one back but I will have no chance in the near future. Also, my letters will be sparse because I cannot write while in the field.

Mom, Happy Mother's Day. I thought about you, but I couldn't even send you a card. Maybe soon I will be able to get something, but you will have to wait.

Love, Daryl

A Hellish Place of Angels

Get Out!

We were said to be acting as a battalion-sized reconnaissance team, part of the DMZ counteroffensive. I don't know what happened to the reconnaissance elements that are normally part of the regiment or division. They were also probably deployed in covert missions. In any case we crossed over into Laos on one of our missions but were told not to write home about it. Reconnaissance battalion is another military oxymoron.

The motto of 2/9 was and still is, "Hell in a helmet." In the jungle this motto was a double-edged sword as it worked to describe our own experience as well as the enemy's experience of us. I remember clawing my way up one hill after another in the hot, close jungle. I was worried about poisonous snakes, small leeches that would crawl up one's penis, giant poisonous centipedes, tigers, booby traps, and friendly fire—in that order. Not to mention an enemy ambush.

The sweat poured off my nose in a steady stream. My glasses were constantly fogged. My green towel was soaked. My teeth ached from gingivitis. Pieces of my feet would come off from being waterlogged too long. My jungle pants rotted off me to a point where my bare ass hung out. I slept on the spongy jungle floor with my helmet around my ass to keep out the leeches and bugs. Jungle rot covered a major portion of my body and I had prickly heat so bad I felt I was dissolving into a waving sheet of millions of shimmering pinpricks of pain and light.

The gnats were the worst. They hung in front of my face under my helmet. They would not leave me alone. They were always there. I would wave my hand through them and they would regroup. I prayed for them to leave. They drove me mad. I would involuntarily scream, *"Get out!"* Everyone understood. It was hell in my helmet.

We were all worried about the snakes. One night my friend Jimbo, a small eighteen-year-old Marine with bright happy eyes and a thin smile of joy woke up screaming and running for the perimeter. He did not stop. We started to yell, "Don't shoot, don't shoot. He is friendly." The Marines manning the perimeter didn't shoot and tackled him instead. He was beside himself. It wasn't a dream. He had awakened hardly able to breathe. A large snake had snuggled under his flak jacket looking for body heat. Most of the snakes were deadly poisonous. No one went back to sleep that night. Everyone just stood milling around or leaning against a tree, waiting for dawn.

The next day we hiked through the jungle where the B-52s had bombed. The two thousand-pound bombs created huge craters surrounded by barren circles of moonscape and broken trees. The craters were too steep and too deep to provide any refuge.

We camped that evening and were resupplied by choppers. We needed water. They refused to land and dropped the jerry cans from some height. The falling cans of water were lanced by the broken trees. The precious water was lost. We went without. I was often thirsty. I carried three canteens of water on my cartridge belt. It was a delicate tradeoff of how much water might be needed and how much weight one should carry.

Fresh Troops under Fire
Dear Mom,
   While I was in the field, I was a fire team leader in the grunts (infantry) because they didn't need a communications man. I had a team of men who had never been in a firefight. We got hit and my team managed to be in the middle of it. I had a hell of a time managing these fresh troops under fire and an even harder time to get them to shoot back.

   Tomorrow we are pulling out for the north.
   Love Daryl

What's the Point?
When I was the fire team leader we were told to man a portion of a perimeter on a hill. The perimeter was soon probed by the enemy

A Hellish Place of Angels

in various areas. My section took fire from a large-caliber machine gun. With terrifying, loud screeching sounds, huge pieces of the large trees standing tall above us were ripped out directly above our heads. Bullets sprayed pieces of earth in our faces. Branches were falling and we were as low to the ground as we could get.

For a while I was the only one shooting back until I got some of them to start. I was very afraid and very alone but managed not to show it, except maybe when I was fumbling with my magazine trying to reload. I told everyone to fix bayonets. I fully expected the enemy to charge our position.

Farther down the line the perimeter was overrun and Marines were found dead with their AR 15s jammed from bad ammo. Most had their cleaning rods out. They were trying to unjam the rounds stuck in the chambers. When they jammed we used our cleaning rods stored in the butt of the rifle to push the round casing from the chamber. The AR-15s, when first introduced, were sensitive to round tolerances. When they jammed, it was like using antique rifles that needed a rod to load powder and shot after each firing.

I regretted not having my M14 rifle and the solid metallic click the M14 made when chambering a round. I also missed the heavy-butted rifle in case of close fighting. However, the automatic feature of the M16 (the military name for the AR-15) and its lighter weight soon won us over.

After sending home the dead, we moved out to continue to look for the enemy. Back in the column, walking with my head down, putting one heavy foot down in front of the other, I was startled by the chatter of M16s, AK47s, screams, and explosions. Some poor bastard up front had triggered a booby trap and ambush.

I wept in my heart when I thought of how they died so willingly, so sweetly. Why did I survive? Others wondered that too and asked me to walk point.

"What's point?" a new replacement would ask. New replacements were always answered with silence.

Everyone dreaded walking the point. In front, one pierced the dark jungle and heavy foliage alone, the tip of a spear, the first to draw blood. I walked the point no more than a few times to do my share and take my turn. There was no choice. You just did it.

One always assumed it was the point man who caught the heat. More often than not it was the third or fourth man. Just far enough back in the column to be lulled into a false sense of security. The enemy could see when one's head would start nodding, looking at one's boots and the dust they stirred. In an ambush the enemy waited, as we did, for the front of the column to pass so the main force could be engaged to maximize the casualties and divide the column. In any case, it was the responsibility of the point man to find the booby traps and ambushes to save himself and his buddies.

When I walked the point I did it way out front. I trusted myself more than I did others. I did not want to be killed by their mistake. I could still see the second man, but not always. I would signal him every time I saw him. I walked gently through the jungle looking at every leaf, above and back. I felt electrified. I would look for a tiny wire or something out of place on the ground. Or anything out of order, like the white of an eye. I would pick up tiny vibrations, a tiny change in the constant chord of the insect symphony around me. I was an animal and felt afraid but alive, very alive. The silent signals to the others in the column would strengthen the connection to the force behind me. A slight raise of an eyebrow would communicate volumes to my brothers. I was silent stealth, invisible, and powerful in the bush.

In the jungle you could hide. This was not necessarily true in the DMZ, where bulldozers and Agent Orange had in many places stripped away any cover.

In Pursuit of the Enemy
5-25-67

I haven't been out of the field since I wrote you I was being transferred. I got this writing gear on a resupply order, so this is the first time I have had the gear, much less the chance. I really don't know when I will be out of the field, but I am now on Operation Hickory. Already we have crossed into the DMZ in pursuit of the enemy. Right now I am only two thousand meters away. I don't know if we are going in again or farther south. This letter was just a quickie so I can get it out on the chopper.

Daryl

An End to the Fiction

On May 8, 1967, the policy changed to conduct ground operations in the southern half of the DMZ. The South Vietnamese National Police evacuated more than twelve thousand noncombatants living within the buffer zone. The code name for the operation was Hickory.

Last week the Marines put an end to the fiction [of the demilitarized zone]. Stabbing into the southern half of the DMZ they drove to the south bank of the Ben Hai, the river that actually forms the border.

Operation Hickory for the first time brought US power smack up against the North Vietnamese border. ("An End To The Fiction," *Newsweek*, 1967)

Daryl J. Eigen

Why US Marines Took War to North Vietnam's Doorstep

DA NANG, South Vietnam—The United States carried the war a step farther north on May 18, invading the southern half of the "neutral" Demilitarized Zone dividing North and South Vietnam. The mission: to wipe out five thousand North Vietnamese regulars using the DMZ as a war base to bombard American Marines to the south. ("Why US Marines Took War to North Vietnam's Doorstep," *US News and World Report*, May 29, 1967)

The communists were violating the Geneva Accords in order to occupy the DMZ to build bases to hammer us Marines. The three red regiments violating the zone were taken by surprise and consequently gave a rabid defense of their positions. They were no match for the five hundred thousand pounds of bombs dropped at the start of the engagement and the Marine and South Vietnam army invasion force. Marines came in helicopters and from landing craft on the beach.

Keeping the DMZ clear south of the Ben Hai River solved only part of the problem. Communist big guns north of the Ben Hai and inside North Vietnam kept hammering the Marine forward bases like Con Thien.

The Marine Corps top brass begged to go into North Vietnam to address the problem but were denied. So we stoically took the pounding in silence ("The Brutal Battles of Con Thien,"*US News and World Report*, 1967).

Lord of the Flies

The DMZ was a sacred mythical barrier that one could not pass without seriously disturbing the fates and forces. Disturb them we did.

On our way into the DMZ we passed an NVA head mounted on a pole. The face was purple, bloated, and stretched out. The skin seemed thick. The eyes were droopy and filled with flies. Under the flies maggots crawled. The rotting human head loudly hailed the horrors yet to come.

A Purely Conventional War
6-2-67

At last we have finished the series of operations. We are now in the rear in Dong Ha. Remember the place I was in when I first landed in Vietnam? It is the most northern "rear" area and will possibly be the biggest, considering they are pushing the Marines north out of Chu Lai and out of Da Nang to let the army take over. The reason for the northern push is to positively secure the DMZ and maintain it. This is the way it always works. The Marine Corps spearheads, fights, secures, builds up an area, and then the army moves in.

This all ties in with the last two operations I was just on. The first we were ordered deep into the mountains and jungle to sweep the area in a series of forced marches. This was Operation Shawnee. I still have jungle rot and sores.

After this nonstop fighting we were shipped into the DMZ where we battled a purely conventional war in Operation Hickory. They hit us with artillery and we them, they shot flak at our planes (from North Vietnam), plus they sent rockets at us. We advanced on hardcore NVA troops dug in with trench lines and bunkers. They blew up tanks attached to our battalion with bazookas and mortared us day and night. There were multiple battalions of Marines on this operation. Friendly casualties were high, but enemy kills were higher.

This is the first time troops have crossed into the DMZ and the first time they, in force, went against enemy-fortified positions World

War II style. I really think that the type of war is changing toward conventional means including definite lines. But actually, I don't know which is better. The guerilla war inflicts little irritating cuts while the conventional war inflicts massive wounds. I hope you will pardon the metaphor, but I am referring to the trickle of casualties compared to the human slaughter I witnessed a few days ago.

I presently have had beau coup close calls and have been involved in so much that I really don't sweat it, if I ever did. [I] believe I will have many interesting stories when I get home.... I am saving them for then.

Now we are resting up and manning the perimeter at Dong Ha. Again I am enjoying hot chow, showers, and a good rack, and I am recovering from very sore feet and fatigue.

Love, Daryl

Note: I was told my fatigue was due to malaria. We were given sulfa drugs as a prophylactic but they proved ineffective.

Operation Hickory

Battalion 2/26 joined 2/9 under the operational leadership of Lt. Col. John Peeler, CO of 2/9, to kick off Operation Hickory on May 18, 1967. The goal of Hickory was to ferret out the two NVA battalions from their fortified positions in the DMZ. The two Marine battalions set out north of Con Thien with the support of two tank companies, Alpha and Bravo from the Third Tank Battalion.

Almost immediately 2/26 ran into intense crossfire from enemy bunkers and well-dug-in positions. 2/9 maneuvered to engage the enemy on the 2/26's flank. We took a blistering amount of automatic and mortar fire. Heavy fighting ensued with our tanks being targeted by RPGs and flame throwers. First "Earth Moving Mama" was hit, with its gunner and the tank commander mortally wounded. Then a second tank joined the battle and was hit and put out of commission (Crumley, U S Marine Corp historian, 2011).

2/9 casualties were very high. The two battalions pulled back with their dead and wounded for the night.

"He Is Already Dead; He Just Does Not Know It"

At one point in the battle for the DMZ we were attacked with RPGs and flame throwers. Several of our tanks were blown up. An image haunts me of a man crawling out of a burning tank with his clothes and a good deal of his skin blown or burnt off. I could smell the burnt flesh. He walked around in shock and confusion. No one helped him. He just silently wandered standing straight up amid the smoke and chaos, his charred arms akimbo on the dusty plateau. We were busy fighting. My FO turned to me between changing magazines in his rifle and said, "He is already dead. He just doesn't know it."

Later they hit us with gas. It is terrible to fight in a gas mask, especially when it is hot. Gas masks make everyone anonymous. It is another small horror to die anonymously.

My experience was very localized, fragmented, and individual as well as being shrouded in the fog of war.

The command chronology for the month of May states, "During Operation Hickory, well-equipped and well-trained NVA troops fighting from fortified bunkers and positions were encountered. These positions had interlocking fields of machine gun fire and defensive concentrations of mortar fire. Camouflaged and placed at strategic locations, they formed formidable obstacles to friendly offensive movement" (Ibid).

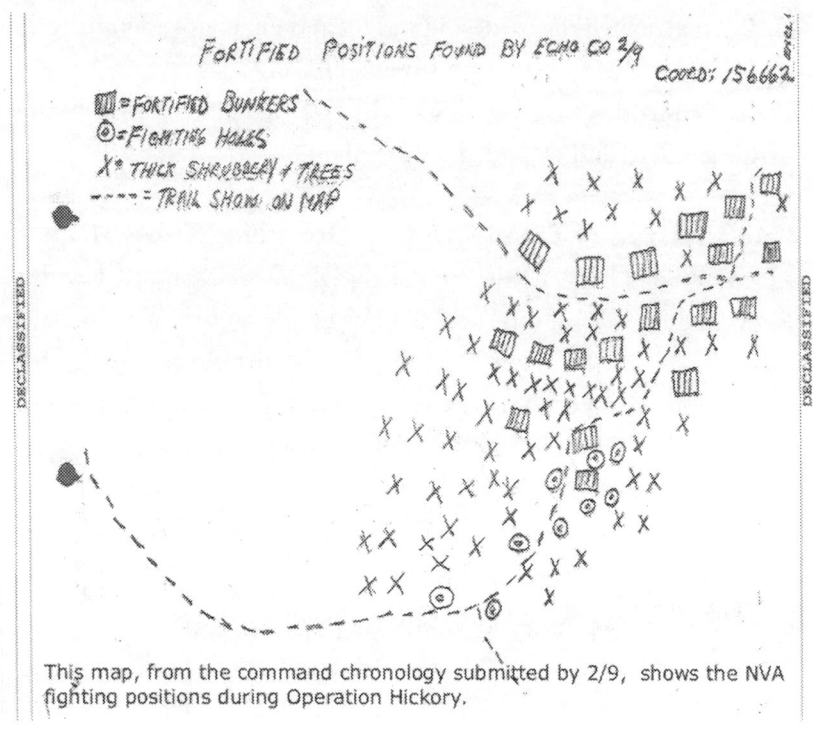

This map, from the command chronology submitted by 2/9, shows the NVA fighting positions during Operation Hickory.

Operation Hickory Enemy Fortifications

Casualties for the operation totaled 22 killed in action (KIA), and another 116 wounded (Ibid).

A Hellish Place of Angels

National Archives 127 GVB-87 A188699
A 2/9 Marine Loses a Buddy on Operation Hickory

World War III?
6-6-67

Tonight, June 5, in the midst of an incoming mortar attack, I heard the news of Israel declaring war. Not too promising of a world outlook, I would venture to say. To us, if the United States stepped in (I understand the Second Marine Division is on standby), it would be just another place to fight. To me, it would be a little closer; but I wonder how you feel with the world around you facing up for war, possibly World War III? Does this seem impossible? I really doubt it, but I guess all we can do is hope for the best.

Right now we are all still at Dong Ha and I am still getting myself together from the last series of operations I was on nonstop.

Soon, however, another one will be up, for it is now in the wind for the 10th. Hopefully I will be gone on R&R, but one cannot say for sure what will happen tomorrow. Again, I am FO radio operator for the 81s. Technically I am in the same status as I was in 3/26 and they realize it is my turn in the field. This is kind of funny about 'my turn in the field' because I would be there no matter what my job in this battalion. As I told you when I just arrived to my new battalion (2/9) and went to the jungle, I was a team leader in the grunts. I was in command but they honored my wish to go back to 81s.

Mail is pretty screwed up and I haven't got any mail from you addressed to my new battalion.

Daryl

Noble and Ignoble Causes

I somehow felt I should have been fighting for Israel. It made more sense to me than Vietnam.

But it really didn't matter. I was a seasoned warrior and I felt competent. I had been through the worst, or so I thought, and reveled in my survival and the numbers of the enemy I had dispatched. I felt my manhood and a connection to the community of men. I was prepared to fight for any noble cause or any not so noble.

Squared Away
6-6-67

I just got off the Repose (the hospital ship) this afternoon. Early this morning I flew by chopper to get my eyes examined and get some more glasses plus get some salve for my jungle rot. It was very interesting but rather depressing with all of those wounded. Most of the wounded are from the last operation, Hickory, which you can read a little about in Newsweek, May 29, 1967.

A Hellish Place of Angels

Now that I am in the rear I am trying to get squared away again. The fourteenth of June I am going on R&R out of the country, perhaps to Manila. Really, though, things aren't that slack right now. We are on operation Cimarron and our companies are all out in the field.

Daryl

Repose on the *Repose*

I felt so safe on the *Repose*. The *Repose* was a beautiful hospital ship that floated peacefully in the South China Sea.

Before I went to the *Repose*, however, there was another evil evening. Just as night was falling we were digging in on top of a hill. There was an opposing hill and enemy troop movement in the valley between. My old battalion (3/26) was on the other hill, complemented with my old 81mm mortar unit. We wanted to mortar the valley and thought it was safer to use the 3/26 mortars because it was a line-of-sight target for them. Everyone could see each other and the valley below. We gave our coordinates and the enemy coordinates. The 3/26 81s checked the readings. We fired a couple of spotting rounds, one long, one short, the usual. We said, "Fire for effect!" They did.

I don't know what happened, but the rounds stepped up our hill toward our position. We were all dug in. I yelled, "Incoming!" The rounds were exploding, one closer than the next. I jumped into my hole and the rounds walked over our position. I yelled on my radio, "Cease fire, cease fire, you are killing us!" The shelling stopped. There was a piercing stillness.

I looked out of my hole and asked, "Is everyone okay?" The word came back that there was one dead. A newbie (fresh replacement) was dead; he had been mesmerized by the deadly beauty of the friendly fire. He had not been in-country long enough to learn the first rule of survival: there is no such thing as a "friendly" round.

I was devastated. Although the mission had been approved by the CO, charted by the FO, and tested with calibration rounds, ultimately I had initiated the fire sequence. I had learned a terrible lesson. It was a shocking blow to my ego, it rattled my sense of invincibility, and it made me feel vulnerable, humble, and raw. No one ever said anything about it. That is war.

The Smallest Battalion
6-12-67

Well, we're going out again, same place we were last time—[the] DMZ. I mean right in it. We leave tomorrow but I don't know if I am going right away because I have R & R coming up in three days. I'll write you about what happens. Would you believe that 2/9 is the smallest battalion in the Third Marine Division because of losses in the last three operations, and we still haven't [received] any replacements? So you know everyone is doing two or three people's jobs and it is quite difficult. Other than this, there is not much to say, so I'll sign off.

Daryl

Sleepy Shark

I quickly made new buddies in the new battalion. One friend was a Hispanic from New York who was originally from Puerto Rico. He would regularly come up to me and say in a friendly laughing way that I looked like a sleepy shark. My eyes were squinted against the sun and the horror. The top of my broad nose was burnt red while the underside was white, and apparently to his eyes I looked like a shark. He just got the biggest kick out of the way I looked. There were no mirrors in the field, so I just took his word for it. A few others called me Hawk, no doubt because of my glasses.

I had a deep sense of solidarity and shared fate with my fellow Marines. Men in battle are very close. Repeatedly facing death and feeling the thrill of survival weds men together tighter than any marriage. There is a silent understanding that passes with a look. A deep connection is achieved that is rarely experienced again later in life by the survivors.

Everything in the war was very simple. There was nobility about the way we conducted ourselves in battle. Courage and honor were all that mattered. The clarity of purpose shined in the eyes of those who were experienced.

R&R (Rest and Relaxation)
6-13-6
US Navy

Right now I am here at Camlo, in Leatherneck Square. It is an artillery plateau and we are security. Today, however, I am going on R & R and I will be down in Da Nang tonight and out of the country tomorrow for approximately five days. I am not sure just where I am going yet, but I will write you when I get back, so don't expect any mail for about a week. Everything is going quite well. We got incoming mortars last night but that is about the hundredth time I have gone through that; so no sweat.

    I'll write soon, Daryl

You Are All Probably Going to Die

It was time for a vacation from work. Could things get any stranger? When I arrived in Manila for R&R I was loaded onto a bus with other Marines and soldiers plus a "Filipino" guide. The guide immediately got down to business and said, "You are all probably going to die." We laughed. "You can have whatever you want here. You have plenty of money and nothing to spend it on. Spend it here before you die. Enjoy yourselves. You can have whatever you want ... boys, girls, whatever you like, just check with me and I will get it."

I spent all three days of R&R in a hotel with a woman and alcohol and tried to sleep and forget. I hired a driver who waited to take me around Manila. I never used him except to go back to the base to catch a flight. But I called him all the time to see if he was waiting for me. Indeed he was. The woman stole my camera as a tip. R&R was as unreal as Vietnam.

Right before I was about to leave I fantasized about deserting and not going back to Vietnam. I am sure this thought crossed the minds of most Marines and soldiers who had been in serious combat and were going back to the same. I thought, *I could live in the suburbs of some Asian city.* I knew if I went back I was going to die. My mind would not let me comprehend how truly dangerous it was until I was out of the country. Nevertheless I went back to help my fellow Marines. I was going to keep my side of the bargain even if it killed me.

Like a Royal King
6-23-67

I just got off of R&R in Manila and had a fabulous time. I can't tell you how much I needed it and I lived like a royal king. I am kind of worried, though. I haven't heard from anybody since I was transferred to 2/9, which was two months ago. I hope you realize my concern.

Also, I know you have read about the DMZ fight and Hills 881 and 861. Well, I was there.

Daryl

Grease Gun

I now proudly carried a grease gun I had won in a card game from an ARVN on my way back from R&R. The gun used 45 caliber rounds, the same as my 45 caliber pistol. I remember feeling cool and salty

A Hellish Place of Angels

about the gun. Out on patrol I got into a fire fight and had to use the weapon. It fired exactly one round. I took the magazine out and all of the bullets poured onto the ground. The spring was rusted to the bottom of the magazine. I felt so stupid for not having checked it. It didn't matter; when the fighting got serious enough, there were always extra rifles from the wounded or dead.

People Doing Things You Would Not Want to Hear About
6-29-67

Everything is going swell and I am back in the old groove again. I don't know what is wrong but I haven't heard from anyone in a long time and to say I would like to would definitely be an understatement. I hope everything is fine and well. There really isn't much I can say, it's the same business. People doing things and people getting hurt, things you wouldn't want to hear, so I'll sign off.

    Daryl

Footloose and Ears to Go Around

I went to the ammo dump to get more ammo and grenades. There was a stack of full body bags that were gray and dusty. Some were open. The white, pasty, dirty, bloody corpses could be seen peeking just beyond the zipper. Near a stack of 3.5 mm rocket ammo boxes was a foot with a boot on that was not attached to anybody or in any bag. It was just on the ground, casually strewn as if it were an empty canister. The boot was nicely laced. This was very disturbing. I tried to ignore it and picked up more grenades. There was also a pile of gear taken from the US dead near the ammo dump. Everyone was too superstitious to use any of it.

    Some guys started to wear the ears of their kills around their neck as a necklace. There was a story circulating of a Marine who went crazy and brutally raped a villager. In our minds it was one thing to kill the enemy and take their ears as trophies. It was quite another to rape and pillage.

Despite these transgressions, or maybe because of them, I began to see that battle is holy. Blood spilled and sacrifices made cleanse the spirit and appease the gods. The small self is destroyed either through death of the body or by being forced into the moment so harshly there is no time for separation. The violence and brutality of war preclude the faint of heart from seeing that the true nature of war is no different than any human reality. God is there. The ground is sanctified. Faith comes from suffering. I went a little mad.

A "Child" Fighting a War
7-13-67

At last I am getting my back mail and believe me, it makes me feel good. I have been in the field for ten days now and I'm quite dirty. I am most proud to be an uncle and I showed the pictures of Sam around.

The only time I have been out of the field is when I went on R&R. You have probably read about the "conventional war" we are fighting in the DMZ. This is where I am and have been for five months. Sometimes I feel that I am in these old war movies on the late show. Fighting the NVA is a hell of a lot different than fighting the invisible Charley I used to fight.

Right now I am sporting a piece of shrapnel in my left arm. I refused a Purple Heart because it wasn't any big thing. You can understand why I don't want one for a petty wound, especially when my friends were killed or seriously wounded by the same grenade or mortar. I have had some close calls and a hell of a lot of war stories to tell. I'll be home in eighty-some days, so I can say a few things without worrying you at home.

A Hellish Place of Angels

The sixth of July we stopped a physical invasion of South Vietnam from across the DMZ. We were hit by gas and some thousand rounds of heavy enemy artillery fire followed by thousands of laughing NVA with blowing bugles. We stopped them cold. Ground troops took light casualties and killed one hundred fifty NVA while our air strikes chalked up a thousand. The next night I saw a jet get shot down by a surface-to-air missile. In fact, I am so close I can see without glasses the North Vietnamese flag flying on their side of the Ben Hai River, the 17th parallel.

Mom, I can't understand why you insist you have a "child" fighting a war. Don't you realize I'll be twenty in twenty days? It's a hell of a note for you to address a man leading men in combat as a child.

Love Daryl

The Enemy in My Foxhole

One night I saw a US jet get shot out of the sky with an enemy SAM (surface-to-air missile). This was mind-blowing in itself.

Shortly after that we got word a team of NVA had penetrated our lines and were dressed as Marines. They were going from hole to hole killing unsuspecting Marines. All night I remained awake waiting for anyone to come close to my hole. I was hoping I would not kill another Marine, but I was ready to shoot anyone who came close, no questions asked. Our holes were pretty far apart, so each of us was very much alone. Usually someone would crawl from one hole to another to check on things, say hello, stay in touch, and make sure everyone was awake who needed to be. Not that night.

It was a horrible night. In the morning several had been killed who fell asleep. My recollection is I never slept again in the 'Nam after that night. I rested, but I was always awake at some level. Any movement would cause my eyes to open. I instantly rose to a hyper state of awareness. That night changed me forever. The black night of waiting stripped me of any remaining guile. My mother was right. I was a child and I just wanted to be home in her arms.

Lord Have Mercy
7-28-67

We're held up now at an old bombed-out church that the French put up when they were here. It's a very good change from sleeping on the ground, but not much. Of course, I am still up here at the fire break (the buffer zone, which is actually a cleared out strip between Con Thien and Gio Lin on the DMZ). I know you have read about all the action up here at Con Thien and in the DMZ. Unfortunately, all this month I have participated in every bit of it. Right now we are destroying all the villages in the area. I am now receiving the back mail and your packages. I am presently smoking one of the cigars you sent and my buddies and I went crazy like the animals we all are over the Danish King pastry! Lord have mercy, is that good!

It is now the twenty-first of July. I don't wish anything for my birthday. There is nothing you could send that I could really use other than the cookies and cigars that you already have sent. The effort, cost, and the faithfulness in which you have sent me those packages is birthday present enough. Also, please don't plan anything for when I get home, I mean parties. I found out today when I checked this church for booby traps that I even forgot how to climb stairs and I am awfully rough-mannered now to be very sociable. One day in October I'll just walk in the house and I'll be there, okay?

Daryl

Foxhole Solidarity
I spent time in a bunker with some black buddies. I can visualize one of them. He was short and highly muscled. His name was Pitt. His skin was very dark. He radiated energy and always had a wide, white smile.

He was a machine gunner and carried the M60 machine gun and wore necklaces of machine gun rounds. I liked to be around him. At night when there was enemy movement he defended our sector with a constant spray of machine gun fire. Every fifth round was a tracer round creating an eerie beauty of red dotted lines of death crisscrossing against the advancing enemy. Illumination rounds I called in lit the area, casting weird shadows across the bare ground. As needed, I would call in mortars or artillery.

With one too many friendly fire incidents, I acquired the habit of calling for illumination rounds first, even in the day. Ironically, I once was almost hit by an illumination canister when the round popped unexpectedly overhead. If it had been a live round I would certainly have died.

When we left the church, the tanks blew the steeple off to prevent enemy FOs from calling in fire.

Into the DMZ
8-2-67

Today we are still in the field and ... are planning to move out on another operation tonight. By the time you get this letter it will be over, but this one will be a dilly. We are going farther north than any of the US forces have been so far. Again, we are going into the DMZ, but this time it will be all the way to, and possibly into, North Vietnam. To show them we can do it. This will be the sixteenth operation I have been on against enemy forces. That piece of shrapnel is finally working itself out of my forearm; it's only a little piece.

Remember Operation Chinook, the one that 3/26 started from scratch? Well, they have renamed it Camp Evans after the first man killed in the [3/26] battalion on that operation. I knew him. But now that I am in the 2/9, I am more proud of it than 3/26 because it is senior battalion in the Nam.

Daryl J. Eigen

I Killed One
8-7-67

I am here in the rear listening to records for the first time in more than a month. I have hot chow and clean clothes again. The reason I am here is because I was wounded on July 29, believe it or not. You'll probably receive a telegram but really, it's not too serious. As I wrote you before this happened, I was wounded twice before but they were comparatively small. In fact, I still have a piece of shrapnel in my left arm from a previous time, which they will probably cut out with the three pieces I got in my leg this time. Also, my left ear drum and possibly my right were blown out and perforated by a mortar blast.

National Archives127 GVB-87 A191240
Operation King Fisher
2/9's Armored Thrust into the DMZ

A Hellish Place of Angels

On July 28, 2/9, my battalion, walked to North Vietnam right through the DMZ. The North Vietnamese army wouldn't let us out. On July 29, 2/9 ran into the worst fight since the two-plus years it has been in Vietnam. We had twenty-eight dead, two hundred-plus wounded, and it took 3/4, another battalion, to help us out. But we killed more than two hundred of them. Our company got its air control party shot up so I took over. I called in napalm from jets so close that some of it spilled onto the road where some of our people were. They're writing me up for a bronze star but I probably won't get it because everyone deserves it. Even the seriously wounded were fighting. I personally killed one NVA who charged at me and a few of my people with an ax, would you believe? I shot him with my 45.

With this air strike and all the mortar and artillery I called in, I have approximately fifty confirmed kills. In the morning I called in sixty medevacs by chopper and we then walked out of the area with 3/4 covering our exit. Too many of those dead and seriously wounded were buddies and very close friends. So 2/9 is getting a well-deserved rest soon and then I'll be home October 6 or sooner.

Tomorrow they're cutting out the shrapnel and I don't know what they are going to do about my ears but I can still hear.

I have had a few well-deserved drinks. So I'll write again tomorrow.

Daryl

The Gauntlet

My battalion, the Second Battalion, Ninth Marine Regiment, walked the area around the DMZ. I can only surmise that our job was to find and engage the enemy under any circumstances. On July 28, 1967, reinforced with a platoon of tanks and engineers we went on a spoiling attack into the DMZ. This action was part of Operation Kingfisher. Our armored column moved toward the Ben Hai River in the DMZ, unopposed on provincial route 606. NVA units were already moving behind us and we would have to fight our way to safety the next day. This exercise and the ensuing battle were to become known as "2/9s armored thrust into the DMZ." Or more negatively it was known as "The Gauntlet" or "Dash to the Ben Hai and back." Take your pick; none of them do justice to the experience.

After crossing into North Vietnam and spending the night unmolested just south of the Ben Hai River, we came back on the same dirt road we went in on. It was my birthday, July 29, 1967. I had just turned twenty. The NVA had been preparing an ambush the afternoon and night before.

In the morning after scouting around and destroying a few bunkers, the column formed and started back on the road. It was a relief not to have to hack our way through the thick underbrush. Because of the bush, the shape of the terrain, and the tanks, it is doubtful we had any other choice. I started to worry that the NVA could easily have registered the road for mortars and artillery. My worst fears were quickly confirmed. The enemy had figured this out too.

We were spread out in a column with limited infantry flanking elements. The column began moving at 10:00 a.m. At 11:15 a.m. the enemy detonated a large bomb buried in the road, wounding five Marines. Nearby, our engineers found a similar bomb rigged as a remotely detonated mine and destroyed it.

The second explosion triggered the North Vietnamese near the road to open fire on the column with machine guns, rifles, and 60mm and 82mm mortars. This initiated a running battle that did not end until dark.

This was to be the start of a very bad day. Some part of me is still on that lonely road. I remember some details of the battle better than the particulars of my life. It is helping to write about it now. It was not the fighting but the confusion, chaos, and loss of order that caused the greatest wound.

The NVA units, using heavy fire from prepared positions combined with the orchestrated movements of other units, quickly fragmented our armored column into isolated segments. The order of command was broken and each fragment had to fight its way through the gauntlet of fire.

The mortars were right on target. The shells started to land on the road and on both sides. The tanks were firing and racing up the road. A mortar series ripped right in front of me. I was blown off of the embankment and onto the road. There was a lot of faint screaming I could barely hear. I checked myself over, and except for my hearing I was okay. I crawled over the embankment to the guy who had been standing in front of me, who was now on the ground. He had taken the round. He was yelling, "Are my balls gone? Are my balls gone?" over and over. I took my K-bar and ripped open his bloody pants and looked at a very large gash on the inside of his leg. The large thigh muscle was just peeled back. His balls were still intact and he calmed down when I told him his balls were still there. I dressed the wound. Corpsmen were otherwise occupied.

Things quickly got very crazy. Fighting was heavy up and down the road. The armored vehicles were useless and sustained heavy RPG (rocket-propelled grenade) hits. The ones who had not been hit were loaded up with the wounded. White and bloody gauze trailed from the top of the tank. I could see that some of the wounded were taking fire as the bullets struck the bodies.

All of the able armored vehicles fled south. The colonel did as well. It was very disheartening to see the tanks leave, littered with the wounded. It was devastating to hear the colonel was leaving and worse to see the tank he was on rumble by. We felt abandoned.

Everyone was more or less fighting on his own. I do not remember how long the shelling lasted, but when it stopped it was soon followed by an attack. I saw the Vietnamese army regulars running across the road, about fifty feet just to the north. I saw a

Marine looking at them and firing his weapon. He was crouching down. The only thing is, he never took the weapon off his knees. He forgot to point his weapon. I was yelling, "Shoot, shoot!" He was seemingly paralyzed. He went down, presumably hit.

Another Marine was running down the road yelling, "My hand, my hand!" I grabbed the hand and looked through the hole in it. One of my recurring images is seeing the battlefield through that hole in his hand. I took out a battle dressing I carried in my cargo pocket and dressed his wound.

Sometime during the fray I heard someone yell something like, "He is coming!" In a trance I pulled my pistol. The pistol went off and my FO yelled, "You got him!" I went over to look and all I saw was a blackened patch that clouded my vision. As close as I was, I could not see the man I had killed; my mind prevented it. My FO said, "You shot his jaw off, and he is carrying an ax." I was unable to see any of it, even though I was looking right at him. Everything else I saw clearly.

I don't remember the order of things very well, but the ground was littered with dead Marines. At one point I spotted an air control radio amid a pile of bodies. I was using both my radio and the air controller's radio and calling in artillery as well as air support. The air support went via a small FO plane that stayed on station. I was doing whatever it took to save myself and my unit. The NVA stayed close to us to minimize their losses from an air attack.

When the jets came in, I told them we were on the road and there were some Marines in a flanking position. Since we were being overrun I told them it would have to be close. The pilot who was leading the mission said he saw us and saw the enemy. The roar of the jet was comforting. The wide gray planes glinted against the sky. The large pods of napalm came slowly spiraling down and exploded in a flaming wall. I just watched in awe. The liquid flame, under a rushing black cloud of smoke, roiled the trees and spilled seemingly close in front of us, not unlike a wave on a beach. The heat from the flames felt good. The hostilities abated some after the air strikes. By 21:00 we could no longer fight and transport our wounded, so we set into a defensive position for the night.

The night came with incredible worry of another attack. I found myself next to a wounded Marine. As night fell, he started moaning. The enemy was all around. I gently urged him to keep still and not give away our position. It was too dark to see his wounds. He said he was dying. I held his hand. I felt death near him and felt as if I might get sucked into a black hole as he was dying.

He died bravely sometime in the night, never uttering any more sounds in order to save me and his buddies. I never looked at his face. I felt a deep sense of grief that I couldn't do more. I felt so much guilt that I had told him to be quiet so as not to give away our position. And I felt shame that I had not asked him his name and would not look at his face.

It had been a long night, but there was no attack. I'd stayed awake all night waiting for the final attack that never came.

The following morning the lieutenant colonel returned with a supporting unit from another battalion. While he enabled us to extricate ourselves from the situation, he did not fully redeem himself then. But not too much later, he was seriously wounded in Con Thien. Blood shared, perceived sins cleansed. So be it.

National Archives 127 GVB-87 A188939
Operation Kingfisher 2/9 Column

With reinforcements now securing the area, I was able to call in the medevacs. The helicopters were coming in one after another. The bandaged, limping, and prone wounded were helped aboard. They all had the same look: dark, sunken, and scared eyes. I lost count, but I evacuated about sixty wounded from this landing zone (LZ). There were many more wounded but they had either fled on

A Hellish Place of Angels

the tanks the night before or were evacuated from other LZs. The battalion was strung out for more than a mile.

When the wounded were gone, some Marines rolled up in a mule. A mule is a light flatbed jeep-like vehicle. Stacked high on this mule were the dead. Faces I recognized were hanging out of the stack on the left and right. The bodies were haphazardly strewn upside down and right side up. Somewhere in this stack was the Marine who'd died bravely and quietly next to me the night before.

One older Marine, probably in his thirties, with a large red mustache and a one-of-a-kind jungle hat fixed around his chin by some respectful comrade, was lying there in the stack, his head hanging upside down, his body arched over the others and with his green eyes open and staring at me. I remembered having looked up to him when he showed up fresh from the states only a few days earlier. I remembered thinking, *He seems cool*. This made it all the more tragic. We lost another one of the good guys.

Before I knew it, I was left alone with the dead, behind enemy lines. The battalion had moved south. Standing in the field with my ten-foot whip antenna, I had the feeling I was being left alone by the enemy to honor the dead.

I could see the Chinook helicopters flying in the distance. I was trying to raise them on my radio, hoping they would make one more stop. Hearing my pleas, a chopper pilot called me, in a panic, saying, "A helicopter is down and is being approached by the enemy." I could see the smoke plume in the distance about two hundred fifty yards away. I said, "I cannot help. I am alone." He was beside himself, crying out, "The enemy is overtaking the downed craft." I said, "I am the only one alive and cannot help." He did not comprehend what I was telling him. The dead and I were witness to this tragedy. Others on the same radio frequency did not respond.

Finally, a helicopter set down at my location and the Marines aboard helped load the dead. Marines work hard to never leave their dead behind. Perhaps more than anything, I am proud of this practice and honored to be part of it. I always took strange comfort in the sacredness of this tradition, even if it wasn't always possible.

The helicopter crew wanted me to go with them. I declined and walked in a daze of fatigue down the road to catch up with my outfit.

When I arrived at the tail end there were stragglers walking with their heads down. My FO was there and said, "I am putting you up for the bronze star." We came upon our captain (H and S Company commander). My FO mentioned the bronze star. The captain turned to me and said, "How are you?" I said, "Fine," in a monotone. He probed, "Fine what?" I was confused. After we had just fought together, he was asking for the obligatory mark of respect and command. I said, "Fine, sir!" At the time it pissed me off, but in hindsight I think it helped to activate my training and reinstate some order after the anarchy of the day before. The door of confusion and insanity the battle had opened had shown me how thin the veil of civilization and order were. I know I saw the true face of war that day.

When we finally settled into our new position only a couple of miles south, I noticed I had been wounded in the right leg, knee, and calf. The hot shrapnel had cauterized the wounds and there was little blood. The worst wound (like most of my comrades) was to my morale.

A Hellish Place of Angels

On the front page of the *New York Times,* Monday, July 31, 1967:

23 MARINES DEAD
AN ENEMY AMBUSH
IN BUFFER STRIP

191 Are Reported Wounded
Column on Way Back
from Sweep into Zone
By TOM BUCKLEY

SAIGON, South Vietnam, July 30—A battalion of Marines was ambushed yesterday as it was withdrawing from a sweep into the demilitarized zone.... According to survivors interviewed today near the Marine strongpoint at Con Thien, two miles below the buffer zone, the trap was sprung by a North Vietnamese force estimated at battalion strength, about five hundred men. From concealed positions on both sides of a narrow dirt road the Marines were following back to Con Thien, the North Vietnamese launched a heavy mortar attack, then charged, fragmenting the Marine battalion, which was strung out for nearly a mile. (Buckley, "23 Marines Dead an Enemy Ambush in the Buffer Strip," New York Times, July 31, 1967)

The article went on to say that the enemy fought at very close quarters and were professional and brave. The enemy fought very close to render artillery and air strikes less than effective. The enemy was so close that our tanks could not level their guns. It was reported that there were twelve tanks of which two were flame throwers and six amphibious tanks. The article also mentioned that a Marine helicopter was shot down.

Wounds
8-4-67

I went down to the hospital today and they are going to leave the shrapnel in my leg. It really is a small piece; the other they took out, and the third one was clean. The old one in my arm is also going to be left alone.

My ears turned out to be okay, no rupture, but the blasts blew in a lot of foreign matter that was embedded in the membrane. They irrigated it and gave me a clean bill of health. Tomorrow I am going back to the field. But in a couple of days they will replace me and I'll go back with the section for which I am long overdue.

I have been receiving all your packages now that I have come to the rear. In sixty days I'll be home. I hope everyone is all right and that everything is okay.

Uncle Jack and Aunt Rose sent me a real nice birthday card. I hope Donna didn't have as exciting a time as I did, but I am sure it was pleasant. The Marine Corps is giving me an eighty-five dollar Purple Heart and the NVA gave me a piece of shrapnel. What did Donna get?

Love, Daryl

Self-Medicating

When I was in the hospital, the doctor tried to get the shrapnel out of my calf. He gave me a local anesthetic and started to probe it with a stainless steel instrument. At one point he thought he had it, but it turned out he was yanking on my shin bone. I felt the tug in the core of my being when I realized what he had a hold of.

After the "Gauntlet" I was disheartened and looked for any kind of relief from alcohol, camaraderie, and/or drugs, as did others in the battalion.

A Hellish Place of Angels

Back in the rear Pitt let me hang out with him and his black buddies. Because I had some integrity in battle and was as outcast as they were, they thought I was cool—for a "pink toe." That night we smoked some very heavy shit, weed supposedly laced with an opiate, and listened to Aretha Franklin. The record player was old and the vinyl records were dusty and scratched. Sometimes it would skip: R-E-S, R-E-S, R-E-S, R-E-S.... Everyone was too stoned to fix it. Finally after an eternity someone touched it and Aretha finished her spelling, R E S P E C T. I felt tight with them. Pitt smiled at me in the deepest of understanding. I vaguely nodded between tokes to acknowledge.

I also spent a half day in the rear with a guy I ran into. He was a pusher and had no discernible job or outfit, lost in the shuffle of records. Originally the powers that be had relieved him of duty for being crazy. It was not an act; he really was crazy, but also very cool, in a catch-22 sort of way. He wore shades, a Hawaiian shirt, shorts, and flip flops. Sitting and listening to the Stones on his record player he offered drugs: hash and opium. We laughed at how silly it all was.

Things were very bad and the post command started to crack down on malingerers. The base commander got wind of him somehow and ordered him to the field. He promptly shot himself in the foot. He was SIW (self-inflicted wound). They hospitalized him, gave him more drugs, court marshaled him, and sent him home to prison. He didn't care. He knew what was waiting for him in the field.

During the last night of our very short stay in the rear, some of us were stoned again in a mutual unspoken pact to self-medicate. There was a mortar attack. Our tent was hit. I came to with dust everywhere and the sky above. I was looking up a golden staircase with shimmering sparkles and there was a muted voice from above. The stairs were going straight up to heaven. There was a bright light and golden sparkles reflecting the light were falling slowly. I had an overwhelming sense of peace and well-being and an urge to ascend.

One of the sparkles came right at my face and landed on me. I was baffled and started to come around. I looked at what had hit me in the face. The staircase dissolved and the sparkles resolved into white small sheets floating down like light snow on a winter's day in Wisconsin.

The white sheets were pieces of paper with Vietnamese on one side and English on the other. The text was US propaganda. The garbled voice from heaven was from a loudspeaker mounted on a light plane that was doing psychological warfare in Vietnamese. I don't know why they were dropping leaflets on our position. Several people in the tent started moaning that they were hit. I was okay and started to help. I did what I could to make them feel better before the corpsmen arrived.

I was very short, as in short time left in country, and so I thought I was going to die. It was a common superstition. The shorter the time left on your tour, the greater your chance of being killed. If one were to believe the stories the probability of biting the dust would asymptotically (infinitely closely) approach 100 percent the week before one was to leave the 'Nam. "I was so short I could jump off of a dime or even a piece of toilet paper and kill myself," we were so fond of saying. It made little sense, which was a characteristic of Marine Corps sayings such as, "Eat the apple and fuck the corps."

Death; it was all about death. It was about being close to death, becoming familiar with death, knowing the ins and outs of death and the beauty and ugliness of death. Whenever death was very close I felt this deep uneasiness, a sticky, smothering sickroom odor and an encompassing golden light. I felt fear so deep my bones were weak.

Over time I was able to realize what a blessing death was. It brings the attention to the here and now and highlights what is important. In Vietnam, it was honor and integrity and helping or being there for your buddies. It is no different in any time or in any war.

We felt betrayed and deeply discouraged during that short interlude in the rear when death was so immediate. We briefly indulged in recreational drugs to take our minds off death, the reality that had been, and the reality that was going to be. The YouTube video ('Nam 67) has the flavor of *Apocalypse Now* with a strong antiwar sentiment and captures the feelings some of us had in the summer of 1967. http://www.youtube.com/watch?v=PD2M4qPoW0k&feature=related

It has a certain emotional truth. Back in the field we had no time for anything but staying alive.

Back to the Field Again and Again and Again ...
August 4, 1967

They are cutting me no slack. Today I am going to the field again. I don't know how long it will last but you probably won't hear from me for a while.

Daryl

Every Time I Turn around An Old Face is Gone
9-9-67

This is the first time I have had a chance to write you in some thirty days because this is the length of time I have been in the field at the DMZ. I will be here for another ten days. We have been through some bitter fighting and plenty of hard times. In the last sixty days I have been in more firefights than the seven months before, which were hard enough.

The rains have started again and I have only twenty-four days left in the 'Nam. My replacement got in today and tomorrow I'll start training him.

There's not much I can say. Every time I turn around, an old face is gone. Every time I take a step, someone tries to shoot in my direction.

Well, soon I'll be home and then it will only be a memory.

Love Daryl

We continued to patrol the area near Con Thien in various sized units. Again we were severely mortared in our positions northwest of Con Thien (Coan, 2004).

NVA Ambush

Another very bad firefight happened in August when I was attached to a platoon on a patrol. We got caught in an ambush with withering crossfire. We were pinned down taking casualties in a clear area between two thickets. I called in air support from a spotter plane. I stood up amid the withering crossfire and marked the enemy position on one side with a "willy peter" (white phosphorous, or WP) grenade. The WP grenade exploded and pointed billowing gray plumes of smoke arched away from the blast in all directions. A piece of WP landed on my flak jacket. The thing about the WP is you could not stop it from burning. Water made it worse. If it landed on you it would use the water in your body and burn straight through you. I was ready to rip off my flak jacket but it stopped burning.

The spotter plane called in a jet that strafed, with their cannons, the side to which I threw the WP. I threw other grenades and fired my rifle in case they were forced to run out of the brush toward us. A fire team took care of the other side. I called in for reinforcements and we were rescued by other elements of our battalion. I was told by the lieutenant I would receive the Silver Star for my efforts. I never did. I was happy to be alive.

After we were rescued, we had to sweep the side the grunts had cleaned up. It was a dense tangle of woods and brush. One could not see more than twenty yards in any direction. I went in with some others to see a terrible diorama. The North Vietnamese were in their hole in various grotesque postures of death. One dead Marine was sitting against a tree looking with surprise at the North Vietnamese soldiers. His rifle was in his lap. He looked like an all-American young family man. Other Marines were wounded and being cared for.

The dead North Vietnamese had been haphazardly strewn about from a well-placed grenade. They were all dead not more than a few feet from each other. We solemnly removed the dead Marine. A body bag was unrolled and the deceased was lovingly put into his bag. One of his dog tags was taken and inserted between his teeth after removing the rubber rim silencer. A well-placed boot to the chin closed the jaw to drive the dog tag between the teeth and into the jaw bones. This ensured proper identification under many possible circumstances. Several Marines carried the dead and wounded to the landing zone, where there were choppers waiting, blowing the colored smoke from smoke grenades used to mark the pickup landing zone.

Then, at the very end of August or beginning of September, the entire battalion (2/9) moved into a defensive position to guard Con Thien.

Part V

Con Thien: "The Meat Grinder"

Con Thien

Con Thien was a forward artillery base just south of the DMZ. Our battalion, 2/9, moved back to Con Thien to provide an outer perimeter in preparation for an invasion. We dug in, but the constant shelling made it nearly impossible to stay alive. For this reason, Con Thien had several nicknames: "The meat grinder," "The graveyard," and "Our turn in the barrel." The myth about being short and dying seemed to be coming true. Ironically, the mound the base was on was called the "Hill of Angels" by local priests.

The following dispatch was written by a staff member at *US News and World Report* who was covering the war.

THE BRUTAL BATTLES AT CON THIEN— WHY US MARINES ARE HANGING ON

Never before in Vietnam—and rarely before in history—have Americans been called on to stand and take it on the chin the way they must at Con Thien. Always before, in Vietnam, US forces have been free to maneuver, chase the enemy, outflank him, attack him. At Con Thien the Americans have been ordered to stay on the defensive, under murderous artillery siege, taking bloody battering day after day. ("The Brutal Battles of Con Thien," *US News and World Report,* 1967)

The enemy used a variety of long- and short-range weapons including rockets, artillery, and mortars. Mostly they hid the weapons in the DMZ, the western high country, and in North Vietnam. I still don't understand why we could not go into North Vietnam and kick some ass. Washington was calling the shots. Bombing could never take out those big communist guns. It seemed like half measures to me. So in monsoon weather one thousand of us Marines on this small hillock, in small dug-out holes filled with red

A Hellish Place of Angels

muck, took a shellacking from hundreds of rounds and on occasion thousands of NVA shells 24/7.

The Marine casualty count was more than a thousand a month in and around Con Thien. You had to be dead or dying to leave that insane mound. Even then it was doubtful you could get a ride. But Con Thien was of strategic importance. If Con Thien fell, then Dong Ha would fall and the rest of the defenses would unravel like pearls on a broken strand. We Marines were not going to hand the NVA the major victory they were looking for. The NVA had multiple divisions in the vicinity of the DMZ and Con Thien. Friendly casualties were high but not as high as enemy dead and wounded from our counter battery fire and the heavy bombing by the air force and naval gunfire. Still the red guns were too far for the 81s. And the bombing raids and artillery could not reach or knock out those guns as they are well hidden or on the move. The only thing that could work was Marine feet on the ground. But that tactic was off the table as a solution. So we took the heat of enemy shelling and enemy ground assaults. Many died for this tiny piece of red mud.

Con Thien provided a fixed target, and the NVA had all of it zeroed in. No spotting rounds were required any more. The enemy gunners would, without necessarily a forward observer, just choose the preprogrammed unlucky area that would get the fire and then fire for effect. But it did not really matter as the hill was so small the natural spread of the rounds, the so-called "cone of fire," would put everyone at risk for every shelling.

Everyone took the shelling or died from it expecting the massive attack yet to come. While our lines were hit often, intelligence sources indicated that the NVA were mounting a massive attack on Con Thien. Since the hill was five hundred fifty feet high and offered a clear view of the surrounding area, a nighttime assault was expected. Other enemy activity in the rest of Vietnam died down.

During this terrible time my battalion, 2/9, myself included, watched over this tiny strategic hill and were shelled until we were all shell-shocked, bloody, and awaiting the screaming enemy hoards.

It Only Got Worse—The Siege (Battle) of Con Thien

No matter how bad it got, I ended up saying it could be worse. Everyone always looked at me funny because one could not imagine how it could get worse. But in the last months of my tour I was never disappointed. It always got worse.

The Tet offensive had actually started in September 1967.... Deployed in regiments and even divisions, the Communist forces were equipped with superb new Soviet automatic rifles, flame throwers, and backpack radios as well as mortars, rockets, and big antiaircraft guns, and they struck with extraordinary precision. Their first target was Con Thien, a small US Marine firebase located atop a barren hill south of the porous boundary separating the two Vietnams. (Karnow, 1991)

About this time, General William C. Westmoreland, head of U. S. troops in Vietnam at the height of the war, had implied that the enemy was in a state of disarray; but the facts proved differently.

On the thirteenth of September Con Thien was attacked, but the enemy was repulsed. We were then relieved by 2/4. My outfit (2/9) was subsequently deployed to the southeast of Con Thien from which we could react if the enemy attacked in force again. As I recall it wasn't the enemy attacks that caused a lasting impression; because we could take action and fight back. Rather, it was the incessant, relentless, and crazy enemy shelling that was unimaginable, indescribable, and viscerally unforgettable. Then if the shelling stopped one assumed the attack was coming. Often the shelling would just start again. It was the worst form of psychological terrorism. Throughout September, inside the wire, Con Thien had around fifty casualties a day. We, 2/9, were now operating outside the wire and taking almost as many casualties. Outside of the wire meant being outside of the constructed perimeter which was made with concertina wire among other things.

Our assignment was to protect the artillery base at Con Thien. The artillery base was well dug in with sandbagged bunkers reinforced with wooden shell boxes. We were to set up a perimeter around the base outside the wire with foxholes only.

We were told they were expecting an invasion again and we were to be the first line of defense. We began to furiously dig in. The shelling started almost immediately and continued numerous times a day for the rest of my stay. Every day I dug my hole deeper. Some of the shelling was coming from the mountain sides, which were not good targets for our artillery or planes. They were too far for our mortars.

The NVA bombarded 2/9 and the other two battalions (2/4 and 3/9) with savage artillery and mortar attacks for the next five days until the nineteenth of September. During the following period, September 19 to the twenty-seventh more than three thousand mortar, artillery, and rocket rounds blanketed Con Thien. (Telfer, USMC Historian, 1984)

We were given a photograph taken from a jet of one of the facilities that was shelling us. It showed a line of trucks that were filled with racks of rockets. The trucks would drive up to two registering posts, fire their rockets a rack at a time until they were shortly exhausted, and then pull away, leaving room to let the next truck pull up. We became experts at hearing the incoming, never straying too far from our holes. We could do nothing but take the shelling. Several times a day the shelling would dwindle our force, swelling the ranks of the wounded and the dead. We were all shell-shocked.

We were not being resupplied because the firing was so intense the helicopters would rarely land. It was a siege. We were dangerously low on ammo from the operations we had been on before coming to Con Thien. Plus, the enemy fire was so unforgiving and constant, we (2/9) rarely were supplied.

> At one point [2/9] were forced to scrounge in their own trash pits for something to eat. (Ibid)

One day we managed to get some supplies in, but it was not rations or ammo; it was, of all things, pineapple juice. The sticky warm yellow pineapple juice was a poor substitute for water, food, or ammo. I was not hungry anyway, I was so sick at heart.

> The constant pounding every day could make you go nuts. You would sit there on edge, wondering if the next round that came in would have your name on it. (Ibid)

Then the monsoons came and turned the dirt into a hell made of red mud and blood. Our holes were in the mud and we constantly bailed water. There was no shelter from the rain or the raining shells. We were Marines so crawling in mud was in our DNA but this mud was different. This mud was pervasive. We lived in mud, wore mud, ate mud, breathed mud, and bled mud. What crimes had we committed where a hell made of mud, explosions, and the constant threat of invasion was appropriate punishment?

On the morning of September 25, at 0715, Con Thien was pummeled by hundreds of rockets, mortars, and artillery rounds. A great deal of this enemy ordinance landed in the midst of 2/9.

A Hellish Place of Angels

The thing I remember about September 25 that really sticks in my mind is a picture of a Marine sitting in a puddle of blood and battle dressings on a poncho with his legs blown off from the waist down. He was numb from morphine and in shock from loss of blood. He was smoking a cigarette very calmly as if nothing has even happened. ... Now you wonder why we called it "The meat grinder!" (Harzel, 2011)

He was either waiting for a medevac or waiting to die. It is unlikely that a helicopter came in time or at all. It did not matter; he would die in any case, just like most of us.

David Douglas Duncan, 1967
Harry Ransom Center
The University of Texas at Austin
Tending to the Wounded

No matter how you made your hole, you would die if it took a direct hit. It was just a matter of time before a rocket would land in your hole. One day a rocket landed right in the door of the CO's bunker, which had a reinforced sandbagged roof that could have sustained a direct hit. The battalion CO and XO were badly wounded. I don't know how many people died. I waited for my personal special delivery of death ...

In *The New Yorker*, a Captain James was quoted as telling a news crew at Con Thien:

> Above all, don't follow me when you see me running down the side of the hill. I like to be by myself when the shells come in. I have this feeling that the round that has your number on it shouldn't kill anyone else—and I certainly don't want to get someone else's round. (Arlon, *The New Yorker*, 1967)

This attitude was pervasive.

David Douglas Duncan, 1967
Harry Ransom Center
The University of Texas at Austin

Marine Running for Cover at Con Thien

A Hellish Place of Angels

At one point, I found myself away from my hole scrounging for ammo and water when a series of shelling started. I tried to run back to my hole but knew I could not make it. The enemy rounds were falling and heading toward me. I came upon an especially deep hole with three guys I did not know in it. I stood above the hole and silently asked to come in. Two agreed but one clearly did not. Perhaps he did not want to be so close to someone so short. We were highly superstitious. I got the impression it was not his hole. The explosions were getting closer. There was room for four. I joined them. This apparently bothered the one fellow so much he got out of the hole in the midst of the shelling. I do not know where he went or how he fared. The others just shrugged. I still remember the inexplicable look of confusion on his face when he left. No words were ever spoken.

National Archives 127 GVB-87 A193030
Marines at Con Thien

Later I took some more shrapnel in my left arm and it became infected. My arm swelled up so I could not bend it. I was given a medevac tag, but it didn't matter because there was no way out. The corpsmen were out of medicine. Helicopters had stopped landing altogether. I also had my orders, as my tour was up. Nothing mattered. I was as short as one could be. I had zero time left in 'Nam but I couldn't get out. This was demoralizing to everyone because they wanted to know that when their time was up they could get out. I was setting a bad example.

The shelling was relentless and unmerciful—day and night, with varying intervals that were never to be predicted. Shells came in like rain. The ground was covered with shrapnel pieces from prior shelling and the terrain was transformed into piles of red dirt, pits, and craters. The turf was constantly reworked many times a day. After a while no one bothered to yell, "Incoming!" Everyone was so tuned into the distant poof, poof, poof, poof, poof.... All who had any chance of survival knew the number of seconds from the poof to the blast. We were intensely aware of the differences between poofs made by mortars, rockets, or artillery shells and what each meant. Every explosion took a piece of me. They rocked the earth and sent dust and mud into the air of my hole.

We had temporary, mutually reciprocal agreements of convenience with trusted casual acquaintances that we would kill each other if any of us were seriously dismembered. These agreements were like casual sex and depended upon what we felt about the other person at that moment and what we felt our chances were at any particular time. These agreements in some weird way provided a bridge to the other side of the shelling.

I no longer felt lucky, but I still loved my hole. It was my surrogate mother, keeping me in her womb. I was alone. The explosions ripped one after another, forever. Finally it would be over. And then it would start again, and again and again and again. I went completely mad. And then it would start again. The blasts and the explosions and the poof, poof, poof never ended.

A Hellish Place of Angels

It seemed every shell I had called in to shell the enemy was now being sent back at me. Such is karmic revenge.

I was repeatedly driven to my knees. I became very close to God in my hole. I was well beyond the bargaining stage. I had already dedicated myself to God and helping others for the rest of my life if only I could live through one more shelling. I no longer had any legal tender with God.

David Douglas Duncan, 1967
Harry Ransom Center
The University of Texas at Austin

Every Marine at Con Thien had God on his Mind or at Least on his Helmet

I felt so close to death I wondered who I was. I had a feeling of being Daryl, but I wasn't much else. I was too young to have really done anything. I had hated high school and didn't like who I had been there. I had a very small collection of personal effects that were in a shoebox at home. I wasn't any of those slips of paper. Most of them were fakes and false IDs anyway that I had made so I could buy liquor. All of my other worldly belongings, including my service records, had been destroyed back in Dong Ha in a mortar attack. I wasn't the clothes I wore, as they were standard issue. The unending explosions had chipped away at the Marine in me. All I was was a son and a brother in a family I had estranged. I had lost track of all of my good friends. I didn't know if they were dead, wounded, or missing. I didn't want to know. I wanted to forget. I began to accept that I was nothing. I was the dirt in my hole. I surrendered to the inevitable.

I had this feeling after one serious shelling that I had died in spirit in my hole. The feeling never left me. During the frequent shelling I was on my knees and bowed, saying the two prayers in Hebrew I knew:

Shema Yisrael, Adonai eloheinu, Adonoai ehad.

Hear O Israel, the Lord is God, the Lord is one.

Barukh atah Adonai eloheinu melekh ha-olam, ashar kidishanu b'mitzvotav, v'tzivanu.

Blessed art thou, Lord our God, king of the universe, who has sanctified us with his commandments.

I had God on my lips every moment of every day in late September. I was Jewish and would be buried that way. I wanted to be buried in dress blues with a yarmulke under my cover (hat).

A Hellish Place of Angels

Soon after I surrendered to whatever would be, I was given direct orders to get out any way I could. I was relieved of all other duties. You can't be any shorter than that. I spent a confused, perplexed night in my hole, relishing my status but lamenting the irony of my having no means to leave. The next day I decided to try anyway. I made a broken run to the landing zone during one quiet interval. There were dozens of wounded and shell-shocked Marines waiting for the medevac that would not come. They all looked so dirty, disheveled, and lost. So lost.

Surprisingly I heard a helicopter coming in. I felt nothing. I was ready to be faked out again. When it landed I went to the door. The pilot said he was only picking up a downed pilot, his friend. He wouldn't take anyone else. I heard myself saying, "Bullshit, you are taking me." I showed him my credentials: my medevac tag hanging on my jungle jacket, my orders, and my pistol, in that order. He started to take off, not willing to discuss it or stay a moment longer. As I had only one useful arm, I holstered my 45 and grabbed the side of the chopper door and just jumped on board. I saved my own life.

David Douglas Duncan, 1967
Harry Ransom Center
The University of Texas at Austin

Helicopter at Con Thien

Dien Bien Phued

According to General Westmorland, head of Military Assistance Command, Vietnam (MACV), "Con Thien had undergone the worst shelling in the history of warfare" (Hunt, "Con Thien the Hellish Place of Angels."*LIFE,* October, 1967). He reportedly also said, "They tried to make Con Thien into a Dien Bien Phu, but we Dien Bien Phued them." Generals have been known to make nouns into verbs, but using a whole phrase as a verb was a new level of art. Dien Bien Phu was the French version of Custer's last stand. It was their last fateful battle the French fought where the Viet Minh annihilated them. That battle finished the French tenure in Vietnam.

I am glad I got to leave because there was one truth in Vietnam: it always got worse. Now there was a label for the worst that could happen to you: being Dien Bien Phued.

A Hellish Place of Angels

The Marines, aided by US air, naval, and artillery support, successfully defended the base (Con Thien), killing more than two thousand NVA soldiers. The battle served to distract US forces' attention from South Vietnamese cities, which were about to be attacked in the surprise Tet offensive. 2/9 was officially rotated out of Con Thien the day after I escaped. Their "turn in the barrel" was up.

Said UPI photojournalist David Powell, "When I think of Con Thien, I get a knot in my stomach and I feel echoes of the fear I felt. God, it could be terrifying" ("Con Thien," 1967).

The battle for Con Thien also made two issues of *LIFE* magazine (Hunt, 1967; Duncan, 1967), including the cover of one and also the cover of *Time* magazine, one of the highest honors of the period ("Under Fire at Con Thien," *Time*, October, 1967).

The famous war photo of Con Thien was taken in September 1967 by David Douglas Duncan (Duncan, 1967) and displayed in the *LIFE* magazine article he wrote in October 1967. It captures the mood and carnage of Con Thien and is the cover of this book.

My mom had the following article from our hometown paper. What must she have thought when she read it? Note: in the title below, of course, we were not soldiers. We were United States Marines. Semper Fi!

US Soldiers Don't Dawdle at War's Hot Spot on DMZ

By Jay Reed: Journal Man in Vietnam

Con Thien, Vietnam—Four Marines did it, bare to their waists except for flak jackets; they ran down the muddy incline of red clay, carrying, as gently as they could, their burden—a brown stretcher with its blue shroud and white straps.

They brought it down to the fairly level circle of red mud, placed it on the ground, and dived for the nearest bunker.... A half hour earlier, the shapeless lump inside the blue shroud had been alive, too—a young Marine who had been cut down by a burst of gunfire from North Vietnamese weapons." (Reed, "US Soldiers Don't Dawdle at War's Hot Spot on DMZ," *The Milwaukee Journal,* September 26, 1967)

Jay Reed was a war correspondent from my home town of Milwaukee, so he had a large impact on my family.

The article went on to try and portray how dangerous it was at Con Thien. He ranked Con Thien along with its sister outpost Gio Linh as the most dangerous place(s) on the planet in September 1967.

He classified it as "a true hot spot of the Vietnam War." And he acknowledged that it was the most forward position in Vietnam. Jay Reed was there at Con Thien so he saw the blood running in the red clay. He heard the pop of the mortar or the distant boom of the high velocity artillery safely harbored inside North Vietnam. He ran to his bunker in the seconds to follow the sound of the rocket, mortar, or artillery shell multiple times a day to avoid the head-splitting explosions. He ran for shelter just like everyone else. When Jay was there he estimated two hundred to three hundred enemy rounds per day hit the very small outpost or the Marine foxholes, such as mine, outside the wire. He was a witness to testify to the truth of the nightmare. After seeing firsthand he acknowledged how the NVA regulars were well-fed, well-uniformed, well-armed, and well-trained.

The NVA threw everything at us to obliterate us like they had the French.

Con Thien—The Hellish "Place of Angels"

It was a rare moment of quiet. Sitting on a sandbag parapet, one Marine wrote a letter home while another, dog-tired but watchful, crouched behind his weapon and stared northward across the Demilitarized Zone. Here, in a desolate, shell-pocked patch of hills called Con Thien—"The Place of Angels" in Vietnamese—a battalion of twelve hundred Marines was frustratingly holed up, forced to submit to bombardment yet unable to assault the enemy's gun positions on the North Vietnamese side of the DMZ. (Hunt, "Con Thien the Hellish Place of Angels." *LIFE,* October, 1967)

We were in clear sight of North Vietnam. Maybe the other side was also driven to its knees by the almost daily B-52 bombing runs

A Hellish Place of Angels

each carrying sixty thousand pounds of bombs. We could see them flying high but also hear the bombs' sound of muted death followed by feeling the earth ripple from the violence rendered upon it. It was also unimaginable to be a target of such an assault. Perhaps it was the bombing. Maybe the monsoons, our insane unwillingness to quit, or more probably the preparations for TET and Khe Sanh assaults that caused the enemy to slack off at the end of September. But they clearly had had enough, at least for the time being, and so they withdrew from the DMZ. It looked like we had won.

But by making hell at the Place of Angels the communists had already made a psychological impact on the US home front where the cost of Con Thien sent war discontent to a new high. (Hunt, "Con Thien the Hellish Place of Angels," October, 1967)

Now They Are Angels

Con Thien made the CBS news hosted by Mike Wallace. (Wallace, September 1967)

All of the operations, bombings, and close combat around Con Thien took its toll on the enemy, as the enemy took its toll on us. No human being no matter his allegiance could escape the reciprocal devastation. September 1967 was the culmination of this mutual destruction. On September 25 alone more than one thousand shells blasted the tiny base.

The end of September was the end of me on many levels. We were all numb to the pain and destruction we had experienced. This numbness would last a lifetime for most of us or until it came smoldering to the top later in life.

When historians discuss the Vietnam War, Con Thien is largely overlooked. Most are unaware of the tremendous sacrifices made by the young men who had to endure the savagery. As to the hundreds killed defending that small piece of real estate, their spirits remain as testament to their bravery. *They are the Angels of Con Thien*. (Hemingway)

The above quote is by Al Hemingway, who was a frequent contributor to *The Combat Report*. A popular author of combat history, Hemingway is a former Marine who served in Vietnam in 1969.

Beth Crumley, a Marine Corps history blogger, reverentially honored the fallen of 2/9 and Con Thien:

There is no doubt that those Marines who served in Second Battalion, Ninth Marines were extraordinary ...

Let us remember those who served with 2/9. Let us remember their hardships and their sacrifices, and rest assured, they will not be forgotten. (Crumley)

Out of the Field

Well, I am finally out of the field. It took a shrapnel wound, my tour of duty being completed, infection, and illness to get me to the rear. If you ask why it took so long or so much to get me out, it is because out of our total battalion of twelve hundred people, all we had left after thirty days of constant fighting was three hundred people effective. And now that the monsoon season is here, everyone became sick. So they pulled the battalion out of the field.

In 81s, out of ninety-six there were only twenty of us left. And when they rocketed us the last four days, we had fifteen people crack up in the battalion with every other man tagged with battle fatigue.

Considering the time in battle, I and a few others managed to stay calm enough to thwart a ground attack and return enemy fire with our 81s. I will be home in about fifteen days so I will see you then.

    Love, Daryl

Hospital
10-2-67

Well, I am still in the hospital in Phu Bai on a medical hold, but I talked to my doctor. He is replacing the surgeon in my battalion Tuesday and is taking me with him and will release me as soon as I get my gear ready.

The day before yesterday they took me to surgery and cut out all the infection.

Last night my colonel and the sgt. major came down and saw me and the rest of the guys from 2/9 who are also in the hospital. Believe me, there are a lot. Also, most of the corpsmen here are from 2/9 because it takes two purple hearts to get transferred here for a "doc" and they are very easy to get in 2/9. The colonel said that I wouldn't go to the field again. No kidding; my thirteen-month tour is up and my wound won't be healed for two weeks. But being in the 2/9, this assurance was necessary to my mental state. Ha! Also, he said that I would be on top of the list for flight dates when I got back because I would be senior, to say the least. I don't know when I'll get home but it will be eventually, and the only thing is time. So see you soon.

    Love, Daryl

I don't know why I was so confident that they wouldn't change the rules and send me back to the field, given the many disappointments I had endured coupled with the deteriorating situation "in-country."

Waiting to Go Home

When we landed in the rear area I was sent to sick bay. I was scheduled for surgery. When I went in the doctor lanced the wound and my arm literally exploded. There was a snake of congealed pus that shot out of my arm into the air. I remember the doctors and nurses saying, "Wow, look at that!" They did some more digging and cleaning of the wound. The remaining shrapnel had apparently come out with the pus jet. The doctor said I had been very close to losing the arm. Later I was told I had a system-wide infection. My wound was packed with gauze, a little of which they pulled each day. I received four shots a day, two of penicillin and two of streptomycin.

I was too sick to leave Vietnam. I stayed in the hospital in Phu Bai. I lay on a cot in a dull haze wondering where the days went. I still didn't feel safe and refused to give up my .45.

Eventually I got out of Vietnam without any further mishaps and was sent to Yokosuka, Japan. They would not let me go until I surrendered my weapon. I finally did and it was cathartic. I gave up war at that moment.

I was still very sick and it was all a foggy memory. I do remember I was in a naval hospital. The sheets were a brilliant white. I was stunned by the cleanliness and friendliness of the surroundings. It was very healing.

Through the blinding whiteness an angelic nurse would talk to me, touch my hair, and tell me I was safe. I was a boy again.

I was so grateful it was over.

Back to the USA

10-5-67
Anchorage, Alaska

Postcard from Alaska's White House, the governor's mansion in Juneau, capital of the forty-ninth state.

No writing, simply an ink stamp:

Compliments of NCO Wives Club, Elmendorf AFB, Alaska

The Works

On the flight from Japan to Alaska, I was one of only a few ambulatory patients. The plane was filled with racks of seriously wounded. Some were so wrapped in gauze and tubes that there was some question whether anyone was home. The plane was very much a military plane with its interior framework showing and webbing for seats. The nurse came out of the front cabin with four needles and works lodged between the fingers of one hand. A roar came up from the group from all who were able. I was laughing until the nurse came to me. All four were for me. I had to bare my ass and take the shots in front of everyone. The guys who were able hooted and hollered, glad the shots were not for them and glad they were on their way home.

Condition Satisfactory

10-7-67
Western Union

Your son Cpl Daryl Jay Eigen USMC has arrived at this hospital. He has been hospitalized as a result of infection in his left arm and his condition is considered satisfactory. The ward medical officer does not feel that your presence is required from the medical standpoint. You may see the patient at any time on your first visit.

Dirty Surgery

I was put on the "dirty surgery" ward in the Great Lakes Hospital that was just north of Chicago and only sixty miles or so south of Milwaukee. Dirty surgery dealt with infected wounds, which most were. There were a lot of people from 2/9 in the hospital. Some were very badly wounded, without limbs, and others were strapped to hospital beds that were supported inside a huge stainless steel wheel. Two were suspended face down. I was a minor celebrity there because I had finished my tour and had apparently accumulated status from being so senior. They confirmed by inspecting my body that I qualified for three Purple Hearts. They had already given me credit for an earlier wound, plus the July 29 wounds, and finally the latest one from the shelling in Con Thien made three. I did not complain, as that guaranteed I would not be sent back to Vietnam. I still was not fit for any duty or able to be released from the hospital.

Great Lakes Naval Hospital

The ward at Great Lakes was filled with rows of beds. The guy in the bed next to mine was nicknamed Inky. He was very skinny and gaunt to the point of hollows in his cheeks. Inky had been in a bunker that was blown up, and a supporting beam had impaled him in his butt, leaving a very large wound. There was a lot of pain, but he had a good sense of humor. A lot of skin had to be stretched using many stitches to cover his wound. The running joke was he was sewn so tight he could hardly blink his eyes. Inky always delivered this pronouncement deadpan. He looked like it could be true. Every time he told someone, I had a belly laugh. That was the best medicine. We were so giddy, so glad to be alive.

There was an all-business, no-nonsense nurse who made anyone who was remotely able to make their beds, complete with hospital corners. All of us hardened vets did everything she ordered without question, as if she were our mother. Every night some of us had the option of asking for sleeping or pain medication. Some crazy vet came up with the brilliant idea that we should all ask for our medication even if we didn't need it. One of us would collect all the extra pills and a volunteer (probably the guy who thought up the idea) would take them to get high. It was still one for all, all for one.

One night a fellow patient who was the lucky recipient of the extra pills was stoned out of his mind. He was jumping around, yelling, and waking everyone up. There were often screams that pierced the night from dreaming Marines reliving their horror, but this was different. It was a persistent disturbance. Those among us who were never really asleep tuned in to the commotion. The nurse was alerted and came into the ward with several orderlies. The lights went on and the guy started his run down my row of beds. I got out of my covers and prepared to tackle him. He got by me and fell on Inky, exactly what I was trying to avoid. I was fond of Inky and did not want to see him reinjured. Too late; he was in agony, his stitches blown. The orderlies were wrestling the wild patient to the ground. Nurse no-nonsense started to lecture us. Inky was taped back together and redressed. And we all had another pretty good laugh when lights were out.

Family Reunion

I finally had a reunion with my family. They all came to see me. I weighed 138 pounds compared to the 175 pounds I had weighed coming out of boot camp. My mother and sisters were crying. I was dark from those months in the sun and I looked like a Viet Cong. I received a lot of hugs, including one from my father—a first as an adult. That was in November 1967.

Epilogue

The Best and the Worst

Thirty one years later, in November of 1998, not too long after I received the brown case of letters from my mom, I asked my brother Chuck what it seemed like to him when I was in Vietnam. He said, "When you left, it was the worst thing that ever happened to the family, by far."

A few months later, in February 1999, my mother died, quietly and sweetly while sitting on the couch in her new condo. This was about a month after her ninetieth birthday party. She lived independently and actively to the end, having just gone for a walk the day before. After the funeral, we all gathered in her house, and each, from youngest to oldest, had a chance to select one of her belongings, in a repeating round. I most often passed my chance on until I heard my sisters in the other room crying my name. In her bedroom, they had unearthed a cloth banner that was painted in jungle-green lettering saying: "Welcome home, Daryl." That was the banner that had been strung across the hospital reception area when I first met my family after returning home.

Someone said the reunion was one of Mom's two happiest moments, the other being when her brother, my uncle Art, came home from a Japanese prisoner-of-war camp after the Bataan Death March. So I was responsible for the worst moments of her life and one of the best.

With my mother's death came the end of a chapter. I was compelled to bring these letters to light to help me understand the impact of the war on my mother, my family, and myself. It was difficult to remember parts of the war, especially people. But as I worked on the letters and filled in the blanks, I started to have dreams. The dreams were not of the horror because that was always with me fresh and clear, but of my old war buddies who intruded into my dreams and into quiet, meditative, or exalted moments. I never knew what happened to them.

A Hellish Place of Angels

Why don't I cry for the lives lost, the families ruined? Where is the grief? It is buried somewhere deep below the fog of numbness that shrouds my heart.

It has taken me all of this time and the rereading of these letters to become aware of the scars that hardened my heart.

Some time ago I bicycled from San Francisco to Los Angeles on the California AIDS Ride. It was 570 miles. On the fourth day I was riding alone, ahead of most of the riders and behind a few. When I cleared the highest peak in the fog, I felt my heart open. Tears were running down my cheeks and I felt a special chill. The fog was thick, and my buddies were there outlined in the mist. They were wearing ponchos over their flak jackets to protect against the drizzle. They were my angels watching over me. I cried for the loss of their lives and the loss of the intricate web of future possibilities, interactions, and relationships that would have been. They said they loved me. My ghosts, my buddies, silently said they were glad I lived. I felt worthy.

Slowly and patiently I bring awareness to these places of deep holding and let them release with forgiveness and care.

Now I see this whole experience as a gift. In its own way it is a path to happiness and enlightenment. My life has been sharper and brighter because I met death and survived. I was reborn. The bad times are always kept in perspective. It seems that nothing could be worse than Vietnam.

I see the horror of war, but I also see the nobility and honor. I am compassionate toward myself, my comrades, and my enemies. Vietnam was an odd mix of gray, fleshy death and beautiful, vibrant life. It is easier to transcend the simplicity of war than the subtle illusions of everyday life. In these ways my suffering is an offering.

I forgive myself, my family, and all who were there, including the enemy. I release the war with its seductive allure and deadly embrace. This experience taught me the blessing of simple pleasures, such as home, family, food, water, and safety. It has taken me all of this time to realize it. For this I am grateful.

I now have a daily spiritual practice and am beginning to fulfill the promises I made to God and to myself in my foxhole at Con Thien. With renewed strength, grounding, and courage I am beginning to live the lessons learned from that deep experience.

About the Author

Daryl is the proud father of Tony (wife, Lori) and Molly (partner, Sarah) and grandfather to three grandchildren.

Shortly after Daryl's release from service he attended college and received a bachelor's and a master's degree in electrical engineering from the University of Wisconsin–Milwaukee with the GI bill, several scholarships, and grants. He invented a cluster analysis algorithm for NASA and is one of the first to have created a software implementation of a neural network. He received a PhD in engineering from Northwestern University under a Bell Labs scholarship. He joined Bell Labs as a member of technical staff and later as supervisor of technical staff, where he created telephone services such as Calling Card Service and the partial automation of collect service. He worked on several other inventions in his career, including the first integration of voice and data on the PC and fault-tolerant optical switches, among others.

Daryl has authored more than twenty technical publications. He enjoyed a corporate career and held a number of senior positions, such as senior vice president of the international division of a Fortune 500 company and CEO of several venture-funded high-tech companies.

After his corporate career he obtained a master's degree in transpersonal psychology from the Institute of Transpersonal Psychology in Palo Alto, CA, and a five-hundred-hour registered yoga instructor certification from Mount Madonna in Watsonville, CA.

For several years he contributed his time, training, and efforts to DePaul, a low-income alcohol and drug rehabilitation center that serves vets. He has traveled the world extensively and has been to more than eighty-five countries. His highest accomplishment was marrying Lucy Burwell Eigen, a beautiful, smart, and loving woman.

He was honorably discharged from the USMC on November 15, 1968. But this was not the end of his experience of Vietnam.

Exposure to violence and Agent Orange has reverberated throughout his life. Not too long ago a doctor at the VA diagnosed Parkinson's disease due to Agent Orange exposure in addition to his PTSD and other less severe service-connected maladies.

Appendix I

My Operations

Below is a list of operations I participated in as recorded in my service jacket. With few exceptions, I was in continuous battle for the last eleven months of my tour. I participated in at least twelve back-to-back operations. This is how they are listed in my service jacket.

- Operation Prairie against enemy forces in Quang Tri Province RVN
    - Dec 11, 1966, to Dec 18, 1966, H&S 3/26/3^d Marine Division
- Operation Chinook against enemy forces in Quang Tri Province RVN
    - Dec 19, 1966, to Feb 16, 1967, H&S 3/26/3^d Marine Division
- Operation Chinook II against Mar enemy forces in Thua Thien Province RVN
    - Feb 17, 1967, to Mar 10, 1967, H&S 3/26/3^d Marine Division
- Counterinsurgency Operations and the defense of Phu Bai Combat Base RVN
    - Mar 11, 1967, to Apr 4, 1967, H&S 3/26/3^d Marine Division
- Operation Big Horn against enemy forces in Thua Thien Province RVN
    - Apr 5, 1967, to Apr 21, 1967, H&S 3/26/3^d Marine Division
- Operation Shawnee against enemy forces in Thua Thien Province RVN
    - Apr 22, 1967, to May 15, 1967, H&S 3/26 and 2/9 3^d Marine Division

- Operation Prairie IV against enemy forces in and around Con Thien
  - May 16, 1967, to May 17, 1967, H&S 2/9/3ᵈ Marine Division
- Operation Hickory against enemy forces in and around Con Thien
  - May 18, 1967, to May 31, 1967, H&S 2/9/3ᵈ Marine Division
- Operation Cimarron against enemy forces in and around Con Thien
  - Jun 1, 1967, to Jul 2, 1967, H&S 2/9/3ᵈ Marine Division
- Operation Buffalo against enemy forces in and around Con Thien
  - Jul 3, 1967, to Jul 13, 1967, H&S 2/9/3ᵈ Marine Division
- Operation Hickory II against enemy forces in and around Con Thien
  - Jul 14, 1967, to Jul 16, 1967, H&S 2/9/3ᵈ Marine Division
- Operation King Fisher against enemy forces in and around Con Thien
  - Jul 16, 1967, to Oct 4, 1967, H&S 2/9/3ᵈ Marine Division

Note: The letters to my mother speak of my participation in Operation Golden Fleece, but it is not in my service record. There apparently were multiple Golden Fleece operations. The purpose of the Golden Fleece op was to guard the rice harvest.

I participated in multiple Sparrow Hawk Operations as a ready reserve force.

Appendix II

Awards and Decorations

There was no mention of the Bronze Star or the Silver Star I was promised. The Marine Corps is loath to hand out combat medals unless it is so obvious that it cannot be ignored. However, I did receive the Presidential Unit Citation with all of the brothers I served with. This ribbon is high praise and rarely given.

Except for the Presidential Unit Citation, the other unit citations (Meritorious Unit, RVN Gallantry Cross, RVN Meritorious Unit), as so often is the case, were awarded after my departure but were awarded for the times I was present. They were verified against the Third Mar Div, 2/9 and 3/26 unit honors matching the times I was in those units. Individuals are to wear the unit citations as long as they meet the time criteria and were members of the unit in good standing. The Combat Action Ribbon is an individual honor and is awarded retroactively. At the time of this writing I have requested that my DD214 form (proof of service) be updated with these awards. The rest of the awards were awarded during my time in the service and are already listed on my DD214 form.

I am proud of these awards and decorations, as they are symbolic proof that I was there and participated with honor among some very good company.

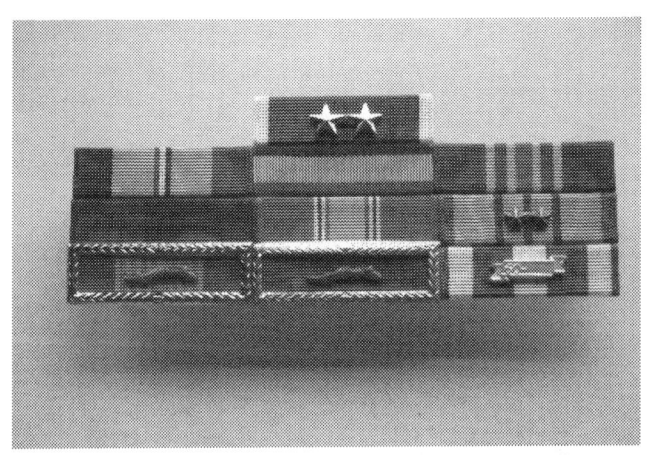

Ribbons

	Purple Heart w/2 gold stars	
Combat Action Ribbon	Presidential Unit Citation 3d Mar Div 1966/1967	Meritorious Unit Citation 2/9 September 1967
Good Conduct Medal	National Defense Medal	Vietnam Service Medal w/ 2 bronze stars
Republic of Vietnam Gallantry Cross w/ Palm Streamer (Unit Award) 2/9 1967	Republic of Vietnam Meritorious Unit Citation Civil Action 3/26: 1966/67	Vietnam Campaign Ribbon w/ device

To properly honor my time in service I reordered all of the ribbons and medals I rated and splurged on a cherry wood case to display them with proper respect.

Appendix III

Tour of Duty Chronology

1966

March 1
The Twenty-Sixth Marines were activated at Camp Pendelton, California, initiating the formation of the Fifth Marine Division. 3/26 was subsequently attached to the Third Marine Division.

By the end of June, Marines were authorized over 278,000 personnel, a Marine Corps larger than the Korean War.

October
The 3d Marine Division constructed outposts along the southern half of the DMZ at Con Thien, GioLinh, Cam Lo, and Dong Ha. The area was known as Leatherneck Square.

December
Operation Prairie.
Eliminate enemy forces south of the DMZ.

1967

February 21
Dr. Bernard Fall, noted historian of the French combat experience in Indochina, died in an explosion of an enemy mine.

The Ninth Regiment moved to Dong Ha, where 2/9 and other elements of the regiment became involved in some of the bitterest fighting of the war, in areas near Khe Sanh, Gio Linh, and Con Thien.

April 24–May 11

The "First Battle of Khe Sanh," or "Hill Fights," took place. In extremely bitter fighting with North Vietnamese troops. Units of the Third Marine Division cleared Hills 881S, 881N and 861 overlooking the Khe Sanh Combat base.

May

Operation Prairie IV—search and destroy in the Quang Tri Province south of the DMZ.

Operation Hickory—2/9 was part of a larger assault group, with six battalions, two special landing teams and combined ARVN actions, to clear the DMZ of enemy forces.

June

Operation Cimarron—a continuation of Hickory.

July

Operation Buffalo—Ninth Marine Leathernecks, including 2/9, killed 991 enemy soldiers during Operation Buffalo while being almost constantly bombarded by enemy artillery and rockets.

Operation Kingfisher.

July 28–July 30

2/9s armored thrust into the DMZ: "The Gauntlet."

September 19 to 27

In a massive attack by fire on Con Thien, the North Vietnamese fired more than 3,000 heavy artillery, mortar, and rocket rounds against the Marine battalion at Con Thien. In response, US artillery returned 12,577 rounds, navy gun ships fired 6,148 rounds, and US fighter/attack aircraft flew 5,200 missions against the enemy firing positions.

This was one of the heaviest North Vietnamese artillery bombardments against American troops during the war and was the first phase of the Communist 1967–68 winter/spring campaign, which would culminate in the 1968 Tet offensive.

2/9, who manned the outpost during the siege turned back several NVA assaults inflicting heavy casualties on the attackers. With the aid of air and artillery support, the Marines turned the enemy attack into an enemy disaster. 2/9 was awarded the meritorious unit citation for this action during this time at Con Thien.

The Stats for the Third Marine Division During My Tour of Duty: September 1966 to October 1967

Note: both 3/26 and 2/9 were part of the Third Marine Division during this time.

	USA	North Vietnam
Divisions	3rd Marine Division	324B NVA Division
		320 NVA Division
Killed	1400	8000+
Wounded	9000	?
Medal Of Honors	5	NA
Navy Crosses	40 +/-	NA
Division Award	Presidential Unit Citation	NA

(USMC Chronology in Vietnam, 1971; Ninth Regiment USMC, Wikipedia; Third Marine Division, USMC, Wikepedia)

Bibliography

Arlon, M.J. (September 30, 1967). *The New Yorker*, p.161.

"Battalion Aid Station" (January 1967) *Sea Tiger* unit periodical.

"The Brutal Battles of Con Thien," (October, 1967). *US News and World Report*.

Buckley, T. (July 31, 1967). "23 Marines Dead in Enemy Ambush in Buffer Strip." *New York Times*, p.1.

"Cease Fire Violation" (1966). *New York Times*. New York, New York.

Coan, J. P. (2004). *Con Thien The Hill of Angels*. Tuscaloosa: University of Alabama Press.

Con Thien. (September 1967). Retrieved from YouTube: http://www.youtube.com/watch?v=oT_fThKZYq4&NR=1

Con Thien Base Camp and Battle of Con Thien. (1967). Retrieved September 15, 2011, from YouTube: http://www.youtube.com/watch?v=oT_fThKZYq4&NR=1

"Convoy Driving Pretty Rough." (February 1967) *Sea Tiger* unit periodical.

Crumley, B. (n.d.). "2nd Battalion 9th Marines in 1967 'Hell in a Helmet.'" Retrieved September 15, 2011, from Marine Corps Association Blogs, HMM262 Blog: (http://www.mca-Marines.org/blog/beth-crumley/2011/08/01/2d-battalion-9th-Marines-1967-%E2%80%9Chell-helmet%E2%80%9D)

"DMZ" (May 29, 1967). *Newsweek.*
Duncan, D. D. (October 27, 1967). "Inside the Cone of Fire." (G. P. Hunt, Ed.) *LIFE, 63*(20), pp. 28–42c.
"An End to the Fiction" (May 1967). *Newsweek.*
Faas, H. (May 1967). "DMZ Something of a Misnomer." *Pacific Stars and Stripes.*
Guthrie, C. C. (February 1967). "Easy Capture For 'I' Company." *Sea Tiger* unit periodical.
Harzel, J. T. (December 31. 2011). "Con Thien the Hill of Angels." Retrieved December 2011: http://www.vietvet.org/jhconthn.htm
Hemingway, A. (n.d.). "Con Thien, Hill of Angels." *The Combat Report.*
Hunt, G.P. Ed. (October 13, 1967). "Con Thien: the Hellish Place of Angels." *LIFE, 63*(15), 42,43.
Karnow, S. (1991). *Vietnam, A History.* New York: Penguin Books.
"Khe Sanh: The Hill Battles" (June 1967). *LIFE.*
Kitel, H. A. (November 5, 1998). *Charley Rose Show* (C. Rose, Interviewer).
MacKenzie, SSgt. N. W. (March 1967). "Street without Joy Lives up to Its Name." *Sea Tiger* unit periodical.
Murphy, E. F. (May 2003). *The Hill Fights: The First Battle of Khe Sanh,* Presidio Press Book. New York.
Mydans, S. (April 1999). "Soldiers Lost but Not Forgotten, in Vietnam." *New York Times.* New York, New York.
'Nam 67. (n.d.). Retrieved January 11, 2012, from YouTube: http://www.youtube.com/watch?v=PD2M4qPoW0k&feature=related
Ninth Marines in Vietnam. (n.d.). Retrieved September 15, 2011, from Second Battalion Ninth Marines: www.2ndbattalion9thMarines.org/index.cfm/9th_Marines_in_Vietnam

Ninth Regiment USMC, Wikipedia. (n.d.). Retrieved September 15, 2011, from Wikipedia: http://en.wikipedia.org/wiki/9th_Marine_Regiment_(United_States)#Vietnam_War

Operation Golden Fleece. (n.d.). Retrieved January 7, 2012, from USMC 1966 H, P 236: http://www.flyarmy.org/panel/battle/66091601.HTM

Reed, J. (September 26, 1967). "Don't Dawdle: US Soldiers Dawdle at War's Hot Spot on DMZ." *The Milwaukee Journal.*

Telfer, Major G. L., U. L. (1984). *US Marines in Vietnam: Fighting the North Vietnamese, 1967.* Washington, DC: History and Museum Division, Headquarters, US Marine Corps.

Third Marine Division, USMC, Wikipedia. (n.d.). Retrieved September 15, 2011, from Wikipedia: <http://en.wikipedia.org/wiki/3rd_Marine_Division_(United_States)#Vietnam_War>

"Under Fire at Con Thien." (October 6, 1967). *Time*, 90(14).

"USMC Chronology in Vietnam" (1971). Retrieved September 15, 2011, from USMC Historical Division: http://www.tecom.usmc.mil/HD/PDF_Files/Pubs/A%20Chronology%20Of%20The%20UNITED%20STATES%20MARINE%20CORPS%201965-1969%20%20PCN%2019000318100.pdf)

Wallace, M. (September 1967). *Con Thien Part 1* Retrieved September 15, 2011, from YouTube: http://www.youtube.com/watch?v=YUy6FHSateM&NR=1

Wallace, M. (September 1967). *Con Thien Part 2.* Retrieved September 15, 2011, from YouTube: http://www.youtube.com/watch?v=DJbwITbnKF0&feature=related

Wallace, M. (September 1967). *Con Thien Part 3.* Retrieved September 15, 2011, from YouTube: http://www.youtube.com/watch?v=IDDDnBB-lN8&feature=related

Whitesides, W. (n.d.). *3/26 Marines.* Retrieved September 15, 2011, from Battalion 3 26th Marines: www.326Marines.org

"Why US Marines Took War to North Vietnam's Door Step." (May 29 1967). *US News and World Report*.

Ynostroza, S. R. (January 1967). "Chinook Will Be Remembered—for VC and Monsoon Rains." *Sea Tiger* unit periodical.

Ynostroza, S. R. (March 1967). "Ambush Well Set by Company from Twenty-Sixth Marines Near Hue." *Sea Tiger* unit periodical.